P9-DWQ-397

Southwest Flavors

SOUTHWEST FLAVORS

SANTA FE SCHOOL OF COOKING

SUSAN CURTIS AND NICOLE CURTIS AMMERMAN

Gibbs Smith, Publisher
Salt Lake City

First Edition
10 09 08 07 06   5 4 3 2 1

Text © 2006 Susan Curtis and Nicole Curtis Ammerman
Photographs © 2006 Eric Swanson, except pages 72, 114, 133, 172, 179 © Gibbs Smith, Publisher

Published by
Gibbs Smith, Publisher
P.O. Box 667
Layton, Utah 84041

Orders: 1.800.748.5439
www.gibbs-smith.com

Designed by Deibra McQuiston
Printed and bound in Hong Kong

Library of Congress Cataloging-in-Publication Data

Curtis, Susan, 1946-
  Southwest flavors Santa Fe School of Cooking / Susan Curtis and
Nicole Curtis Ammerman.—1st ed.
      p. cm.
  Includes bibliographical references and index.
  ISBN 1-58685-697-9
  1. Cookery, American—Southwestern style. 2. Santa Fe School of Cooking.
I. Ammerman, Nicole Curtis. II. Santa Fe School of Cooking. III. Title.

TX715.2.S69C884 2006
641.5979—dc22

                              2005025787

This book is dedicated to David Ballantyne Curtis, husband and father extraordinaire.

Contents

Acknowledgments

This cookbook is a collaborative effort of many talented people. First and foremost we would like to thank the chefs who developed the recipes. This group of chefs is wonderful to work with, fun to be around and have so much information to share with guests at The Santa Fe School of Cooking, but also with all of us who work around them. We appreciate their hard work and enthusiasm for their profession. It is also important to recognize chefs that are no longer at the school but who have contributed recipes, ideas and stories that will always live on. Jeff Pufal, Janet Mitchell and Allen Smith are some who are deeply missed.

We send our deepest thanks to the terrific people who have supported The Santa Fe School of Cooking over the years. We have so many wonderful guests who have come through our doors. Many have become great friends who have shared in the events of our small family business. Thank you for supporting our vision.

We have been lucky to have such a wonderful staff. Noe Cano has been our kitchen manager and sous chef for nine years. We have watched him learn from all the chefs who have come through the doors and, in turn, he now teaches us all many things about food and cooking. Susan Thomas has been with us for nine years and always gives 100 percent in providing terrific customer service and ever smiles while doing the sometimes mundane jobs. Susie McClendon is always keeping the sales floor full, neat and orderly, and all the while keeping us happy with her wonderful, relaxed personality. Christiann Stapf played an important role in formatting these recipes and it is much appreciated. Kathi Long and Rocky Durham were both very important in helping with recipe testing, food styling and other important details.

Thanks to our suppliers, who work hard to find us the best New Mexican ingredients possible so that we can offer them to you. Many work extra long days in the busy season to get the products to us. In particular, we would like to acknowledge Martin Dobyns and Missy Agnew, who always go the extra mile to help us out. Also, to our farmers who are unique and uncommon in this day and age in trying to keep alive traditional methods of producing and harvesting foods.

One of our favorite things about doing this book was getting to work with Eric Swanson. His photographs are simply stunning. His attention to detail is unsurpassed and he is so much fun to be around. Dimity McDowell Davis helped tremendously when the big crunch came to get this book completed.

Finally, thank you to all of our friends who tasted the food with us when we were testing these recipes. It is a rough job, but someone has to do it! Our family members were the main source of guinea pigs and our appreciation goes to Mike Ammerman, David Curtis, Kristen Krell, Tree Krell and, of course, Dylan Krell and Haley Ammerman. Friends who helped with this process include Charlie and Dianne Nylander, Bill and Cheryl Jamison, Eddie and Mirabai Daniels, Anne and Witter Tidmore, Tom and Heidi Tilton, Caroline and Bill Burnett, Jerry Allen, Suzanne Valenzuela, Tiffany St. Peter, Raney St. Peter, Jason Auslander and Patty Romero.

FOREWORD

The Santa Fe School of Cooking originated out of an extremely intense midlife crisis. In 1989, I found myself experiencing empty nest syndrome. My oldest daughter, Nicole, was in college and my youngest, Kristen, was about to enter college. Although I had worked for years, the dread of this major life change and the anticipated void was overwhelming. What was a mother to do? My solution was to start The Santa Fe School of Cooking, which is now considered my third child. All of the nurturing I had smothered on my children shifted to starting the school.

The shear terror of failure and its consequences on my family motivated me to put every ounce of energy into the school. The cliché "blood, sweat and tears" aptly describes what it takes to start a business. As often happens, the hectic pace can cause burnout. This is where I found myself after five years. Fortunately, Nicole had graduated from college in business and had a year's work experience under her belt. With some trepidation on both parts, she decided to return to Santa Fe as day-to-day manager of the SFSC.

This provided me with much-needed support. Within a few years, I had relinquished major responsibility to her.

Fortunately, we found that we loved working together. Our strengths and weaknesses complemented each other's and I was able to spend more time on what I really love to do: visioning new projects and directions for the business.

The first SFSC cookbook was near completion at the time Nicole came on board as manager. This new cookbook reflects not only the recipes developed since the first book, but also the trends and changes which are partly influenced by Nicole's presence. We hope you enjoy the recipes and stories within this book and, most importantly, we hope you will visit us at the school and market.

Buen Provecho,
Susan Curtis

INTRODUCTION

WELCOME TO THE SANTA FE SCHOOL OF COOKING

The Santa Fe School of Cooking staff from left to right: (front) James Campbell Caruso, Eddie Lyons, Kathi Long, Susan Curtis, Nicole Curtis Ammerman, Lois Ellen Frank, Daniel Hoyer; (back) Rocky Durham, Carmen Rodriguez, Steve Cooper, and Noe Cano.

Over the years, the mission of the Santa Fe School of Cooking has always been to celebrate and promote the rich historic traditions and food of Santa Fe and its surroundings. Unlike many communities in the United States, Santa Fe truly boasts a regional cuisine reflecting the mix of cultures—Native American, Spanish, Mexican and Anglo. The first classes offered at the school focused on traditional New Mexican cuisine with dishes such as enchiladas, beans, posole and green chile stew. As the school grew, a broader mix of classes was offered, reflecting the ragout of cultures in this area. Spanish tapas, Mexican cuisine, Native American foods, and contemporary Southwestern classes offered dishes such as Shrimp Escabeche with Black Olives and Mint, Roast Pork Loin with Red Chile Mole, and Goat Cheese Enchiladas with Tomatillo Sauce. Still within the focus of our mission, classes using southwestern ingredients were developed for healthier and lighter menus and, recently, low-carbohydrate diets.

The format of classes at the school is typically demonstration style and encourages lively interaction between the audience and chef. However, we have added hands-on classes where participants can make their own chile sauces, tortillas and quesadillas. A hands-on class proving to be quite popular is the family class, where multiple generations come together to cook. This idea originated from requests for activities for family reunions. The class provides the opportunity for parents, grandparents, and kids to spend time in the kitchen together and get a taste of the local cuisine. Corporate-team-building cooking classes provide an opportunity for coworkers to succeed together in a different environment: the kitchen. And finally, one of our most popular classes is the Farmers Market class where participants help choose ingredients at the market and return to the school to prepare an impromptu lunch.

Like our classes, the market adjacent to the school
also promotes the traditions and food of this area. There are over 600
products available—most made in New Mexico. You will find many jars of
salsa, rubs and dips as well as rustic juniper cutting boards, handmade
pottery, cooking utensils and much, much more.

Like our classes, the market adjacent to the school also promotes the traditions and food of this area. There are over 600 products available—most made in New Mexico. You will find many jars of salsa, rubs and dips as well as rustic juniper cutting boards, handmade pottery, cooking utensils and much, much more. The school has its own product line focusing primarily on unique ingredients indigenous to this area, such as chicos, posole, blue corn, cedron (juniper berries) and a variety of chiles. Most items in the market are available through our mail-order catalog or on our Web site, providing cooks around the world access to these unusual products.

In the pages that follow, we introduce you to some of the unique individuals involved in the school—including some of the farmers who grow products for us, local vintners and, of course, the chefs who create the recipes. In our classes, we encourage chefs to use the recipes only as a starting point, and then allow guests to witness the creative process in action. It is our belief that this format offers a more interesting and accurate learning experience than simply following a recipe. With nine chefs on hand, you can imagine that some write more detailed instructions than others. Thus, the recipes are always evolving. We have chosen what we consider the best interpretation of each dish and made sure they work for the home cook. We strive to reach the middle ground and provide a simple and understandable recipe that anyone can follow. Our hope is that you will use these recipes to explore this most multicultural cuisine.

Chef Biographies

Noe Cano, kitchen manager and sous chef for more than nine years, is an invaluable asset to the chefs that he assists.

James Campbell Caruso is the Executive Chef for El Farol, one of Santa Fe's favorite restaurants specializing in Spanish tapas. He recently completed a cookbook called *El Farol: Tapas and Spanish Cuisine*.

Steve Cooper has owned a restaurant and a catering business and is currently the director of the culinary arts program at the Santa Fe Community College.

Rocky Durham, a graduate of the Western Culinary Institute in Portland, Oregon, is a native Santa Fean who is a TV host and syndicated food columnist, *Plates Across the States*.

Enrique Guerrero is the newest addition to the staff. His impressive background includes being the personal chef for the president of Mexico for four years. He is currently the Executive Chef at The Galisteo Inn.

Lois Ellen Frank is our Native American specialist. She authored her own cookbook, *Foods of the Southwest Indian Nations,* which won a James Beard award in 2003.

Daniel Hoyer leads gastronomic adventure tours through Mexico. His first solo cookbook was *Culinary Mexico: Authentic Recipes and Traditions.*

Kathi Long combines demanding careers as a personal chef, food-service consultant and food stylist. She is also the author and coauthor of five cookbooks.

Eddie Lyons began his career by apprenticing with a French chef. He has been the chef at several of Santa Fe's top restaurants, including The Pink Adobe and The Galisteo Inn.

Carmen Rodriguez brings to the school over twenty years' experience in the food-service industry and is currently the Executive Chef at the long-standing Italian restaurant Pranzo Italian Grill in Santa Fe.

CHILE

Chile is the foundation of Southwestern cuisine. It is designated as the "state vegetable" of New Mexico, though it is actually a fruit. The nearly infinite variety and complexity of flavors found in chiles are what makes our food so special and unique.

The characteristic for which chiles are best known is their heat. This fiery sensation is caused by capsaicin, a potent chemical compound that survives both cooking and freezing processes. Burns caused by contact with the capsaicin can be painful and can cause serious injury to the eyes. We recommend wearing gloves, but if you forget, rub oil on your hands. Oil works better than water because capsaicin is oil soluble but is not miscible in water. If you eat chile that burns your mouth, the best solution is to eat or drink dairy products. A glass of milk or a side of sour cream will help cool things down. Despite the potential dangers, chile remains popular precisely because the fiery sensation we feel on our tongue causes the brain to release endorphins—promoting a sense of pleasure and well-being. Capsaicin also exhibits medical benefits as a decongestant and ointment to relieve joint pain.

There are around two hundred varieties of chile, each with its own distinctive character. All members of the *Capsicum* genus, or the culinary varieties, derive their distinct characteristics—shape, color, heat and flavor attributes—from a myriad of growing conditions such as soil, climate, length of time on the vine and gene selection. Thus, like grapes, the same chile cultivar grown in two different places will not taste the same.

Chiles are available fresh, frozen, dried, canned and powdered depending on the type of chile. In New Mexico, frozen chile is usually available year-round and, in fact, any self-respecting chile addict has a freezer full of plastic bags stuffed with roasted green chile. Outside the Southwest chile may be difficult to find off-season. Anaheim chiles from California are often available during the winter months, but these are not the same as true New Mexico Hatch or Chimayo chiles. The harvest

Chiles are good for you.
They are low in calories, low in sodium and cholesterol-free.
They are also very high in vitamins A and C and a good source of
vitamin E, potassium and folic acid.

season in New Mexico lasts only a few months, beginning in late July. Nonetheless, many chiles are available dried in specialty food markets; when purchasing you want to look for chiles that are soft and pliable. Chiles in jars or cans are the easiest to find across the United States, although they are usually the poorest quality. Pure chile powders are made exclusively from one type of chile. A good-quality chile powder should have a deep, rich color and be slightly lumpy, which indicates that the natural oils have not evaporated and are still fresh.

Chiles are good for you. They are low in calories, low in sodium and cholesterol-free. They are also very high in vitamins A and C and a good source of vitamin E, potassium and folic acid.

Although many chiles are very hot—sometimes so hot that the heat masks other flavors—there are many varieties that offer rich and wonderful flavor profiles, sure to enhance nearly any dish or cuisine. Following is a list of our favorite chiles used at the Santa Fe School of Cooking:

Aji Amarillo: This is a very spicy South American chile that is quite common in Peru and neighboring countries but relatively unknown in the Southwest. It is orange in color and wrinkled, measuring about 4 inches in length. It has a fruity flavor and makes beautiful sauces because of its unusual color.

Ancho: The ancho is highly esteemed in Mexico, where it accounts for approximately one-fifth of all chiles consumed there. Ancho, the dried form of the green Poblano, literally means "wide chile pepper." It is a deep reddish brown, flat, heart-shaped chile measuring about 5 inches in length. It is quite mild in heat and can be described as a sweet chile with tones of fruit, coffee and licorice.

Cascabel: A dried, dark reddish brown chile with a smooth, tough skin and a round shape about 1 1/2 inches in diameter. In Spanish, *cascabel* means "rattle," and the chile is so named because of the sound the seeds make inside the dried pepper. It has medium heat with a slightly acidic, woodsy quality.

Habanero: Its reputation as the hottest chile is responsible for its fame. It can be used fresh or dried and comes in a variety of colors from red to orange to yellow, although orange seems to be the most popular. It is lantern shaped, measuring about 1 1/2 to 2 inches in length. Habaneros have tropical fruit flavors and are most commonly associated with barbecue rubs and marinades. They are used extensively in Caribbean cooking, where they are called Scotch Bonnets.

Chile Caribe: This is simply the crushed form of New Mexican dried red chile pods along with the seeds.

Chipotle: This is the dried and smoked form of a fresh jalapeño chile. Dusty brown in color, it has gained enormous popularity in recent times because of its rich, smoky flavor and good solid heat. It is about 2 inches long with ridged, wrinkly skin. About 20 percent of all jalapeños grown in Mexico are used for the production of chipotle.

Chipotles en adobo: Chipotle chiles come in cans or jars in a sauce of tomatoes, oil, vinegar, garlic, onion and spices. This is great for adding to soups, stews and beans. It was previously difficult to find, but we liked it so much that we decided to produce it ourselves under our in-house label!

Chipotle seasoning: This is another product that we package ourselves because we are such big fans! It is a combination of chipotle chile powder, garlic, sugar and salt that is great used as a rub on meats or mixed with sour cream to create a great dip.

De Arbol: A dried, bright red chile measuring 2 to 3 inches in length. It is very hot with intense flavor and is often the primary heat source in table sauces and chile oils. In Spanish, the name means "treelike," an allusion to the lush plant with woody stems.

Guajillo: This dried red chile pod looks similar to a dried New Mexican pod but is smaller and smoother in texture. One of the most common cultivars in Mexico, it is fairly mild with hints of berry.

New Mexico Green Chile: These fresh chiles, often referred to as Hatch chiles, range between 6 and 12 inches in length and are generally a medium green in color. Hatch is a small town in southern New Mexico that has become famous for its chile production, especially green chile. Green chiles are always roasted and peeled and are the base of any New Mexican green chile sauce. The heat varies enormously, as there are many cultivars within the New Mexico green chile family. For example, the NuMex Big Jim is a large variety that is great for making chiles rellenos (stuffed chiles). The New Mexico 6-4 is the most popular commercially grown variety. The Sandia and the aptly named Barker Hot appeal to those who truly enjoy a good burn. Anaheims may be substituted; however they don't exhibit the sweet earthiness that has made the New Mexican green chile so famous.

Green Chile Powder: This is not as common as the fresh green chile mentioned, as most green chile is used fresh or frozen in our area. In order to get the powder, the green chiles are picked early, before they turn red, and are dried, seeded, stemmed and ground to a fine powder. It is usually fairly mild, as primarily the mild New Mexico 6-4 is used to make the powdered form.

Green Chile Dip: This is a mix we sell in the store and have trouble keeping on the shelves! It is a blend of Big Jim green chile powder, garlic, sugar and salt. Mix it with sour cream for a fantastic dip!

Jalapeño: This is the most famous and most widely used chile in the U.S. It is 2 to 3 inches long and is a medium to dark green with a medium heat (although the heat can vary greatly from chile to chile). Jalapeños are very versatile and can be used in salsas, pickled in escabeche, diced and used as toppings or even stuffed.

Morita. Another type of dried, smoked jalapeño chile that is reddish brown in color. It measures 1 to 2 inches in length and has a sweet, smoked flavor with hints of tobacco.

Pasilla: This chile is also known as the chile negro. Pasilla is a dried chile that is fairly mild, 5 to 6 inches long with flavors of berry and herbs. It literally means "little raisin" and is most famously used in making traditional moles.

Poblano: This is one of the most popular chiles used in Mexico, it is the fresh form of the ancho chile. Poblanos are 4 to 5 inches long but 2 1/2 to 3 inches wide, which makes them very good chiles for making rellenos, as they are easy to stuff. Poblanos are deep green with an almost black tinge to the flesh; they are always roasted and peeled before use.

Serrano: Fresh, small green chile, cylindrical in shape and measuring approximately 1 to 2 inches long. It is a crisp, hot chile used mostly in salsas. It can be found red from time to time, which makes the flavor slightly sweeter. Jalapeño can be substituted when serrano can't be found.

New Mexico Red Chile: The form of the green chile that has ripened to its red state and dried. As is the case with the New Mexico green chile, New Mexico red chile encompasses several varieties of chile and the heat can vary greatly. They are 5 to 7 inches in length with an earthy taste. The traditional method for storing these chiles is to tie them in a long bunch called a *ristra,* which has become a symbol of the culture of the state.

Red Chile Powder: This is the dried version of the New Mexico green chile that has ripened (turned red) and been ground into a pure powder with no additional ingredients. It is sometimes referred to as *molido*, which just means milled, or Chimayo chile. Chimayo is a village north of Santa Fe that grew a medium hot variety of chile that became so well known that many people often refer to any red chile as Chimayo.

ROASTING CHILES

Each year in late summer and early autumn, residents of New Mexico embark upon an annual culinary ritual: roasting and storing fresh green chile for the months ahead. From Santa Fe to the Mesilla Valley, a pungent, smoky aroma permeates the air and self-described chile addicts take deep, joyful breathes. The scent is difficult to describe—something akin to the burning of leaves once common but also vegetal, even slightly acrid at times. However it is described, this scent is uniquely Southwestern and stands as one of the surest signs that you have arrived in chile country.

We always roast green chiles before we use them. The skin on the outside of the chile is thick, plasticy and bitter and needs to be removed. Essentially what you are doing is blistering a whole chile over a heat source, then peeling off the blackened skin. It is key to use the highest, most direct heat possible for the shortest amount of time. In essence, blistering the outside (skin) while leaving the inside (flesh) plump and fresh. The amount of charring necessary to

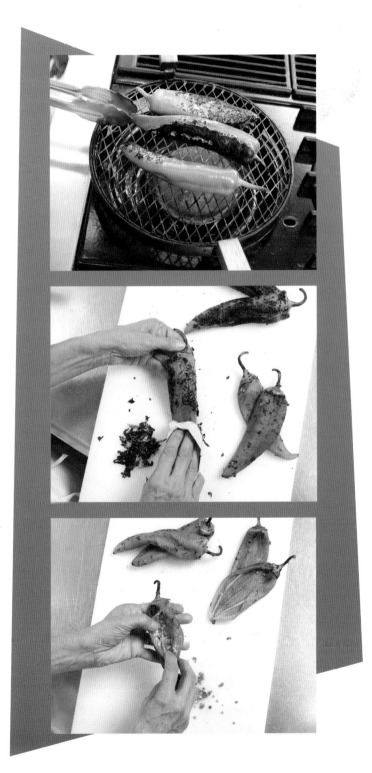

remove the skin can be surprising to anyone who has never attempted this process before. You really do need to blacken the majority of the chile's flesh in order to remove the skin. But the flesh is not burned just because it is black. Blacken the chiles carefully, as over-roasting will result in lacey flesh that is very delicate and difficult to handle. Here are instructions for doing so:

1. Roast whole chile over heat source until thoroughly charred, turning with tongs to get all sides.

Let the chile sweat or rest for 5 minutes after roasted, either wrapped in plastic or sealed in a closed zipper-lock bag.

2. Gently pull away charred skin. You can wipe it off with a towel. If having a hard time, run a slow stream of cold water and place chile in water to help remove the skin. Some chefs will argue, however, that when using this method you wash away some of the important oils and flavors from the chile.

3. Either with a knife or your fingers, remove inner ribs and seeds. If using the chile for rellenos, be sure to keep the chile intact and make a careful incision in one side.

NOTE: If you are roasting a large quantity of green chiles meant to be frozen, you may freeze the chiles after roasting and peel them later when pulled out and thawed. The skin actually comes off easier at this point.

FREQUENTLY ASKED QUESTIONS

We figured the best way to help de-mystify this style of cuisine for the person who hasn't been to our school is to share with you some of the most frequently asked questions at the Santa Fe School of Cooking.

What is the difference between Mexican and New Mexican food?

New Mexican food is simpler and more straight-forward than Mexican cooking. This is due to New Mexico's relative isolation and climate. The lack of trade and short growing season and/or arid climate limits the variety in New Mexico. New Mexicans have created variety through different preserving and cooking techniques. Mexico is a huge region whose food varies from state to state as a result of geography. Both cuisines have Spanish and Native American influences, but Mexican food has a lot more variety simply due to its size and geographic diversity. For example, traditional New Mexican food relies almost exclusively on the locally grown red and green chiles, whereas hundreds of varieties of chiles are grown in Mexico.

Which is hotter, red or green chile?

Both. Or neither. It all depends on the specific variety of chile plant. Some green chiles are fiery while others are mild. The same is true of red chile. However, there is no universal truth that one is always going to be hotter than the other. One thing to note, however, is that dry chiles have less volume; therefore, often more red chiles (which are dried) are used in the same volume of sauce or salsa than green, sometimes causing red to be hotter.

What should I do if I've eaten chile that is too hot?

Chiles are hot because of the presence of an oil called capsaicin. Like all oils, it does not mix or dissolve in water. That is why water or iced tea do not wash away the burn of hot chile. Oils, however, do like to blend with other oils. Dairy fat is a type of oil present in whole milk, sour cream and cheese. These will help "lift" the capsaicin from your tongue. Citric acid also has oil-cutting properties, so biting into a wedge of lime can be an effective and tasty method of beating the burn. Carbohydrates, especially sugars (honey), also help alleviate the heat sensation of chiles.

If a recipe calls for pods, in what quantity can I substitute powder?

Obviously, the answer to this question depends on what type of chile you are using, as chiles vary greatly in size. However, a good rule of thumb is 1 dried chile equals between 1/2 teaspoon to 1 tablespoon of powder. For example, a dried ancho chile yields one tablespoon of powdered chile.

Are posole and hominy the same thing?

Posole and hominy are essentially the same thing. Posole uses dry corn kernels that are boiled in a hydrate lime solution for approximately one hour, or until the hulls come off. They are then rinsed and washed thoroughly to remove the lime solution. The kernels are then placed on drying racks and turned to prevent molding. Hominy goes through the same process of cooking with the lime. Hominy seems to be prevalent in the South and is commonly found canned. Posole is found primarily in the Southwest and is usually found dried or frozen, but not canned.

What is a piñon nut?

Piñon nuts ripen in the crevices of pinecones in the piñon trees that dominate the landscape of northern New Mexico. Piñon nuts have been hand-gathered in the wild since the days of the earliest Indians. They are quite expensive as there are limited mechanized ways to shell them. Piñon nuts have a high oil content that makes them preferable to Italian pignoli or Chinese pine nuts. In the last few years, the piñon trees of the Southwest suffered a terrible bark beetle infestation that has destroyed as much as 85 percent of the trees, therefore making good piñon nuts that much harder to find and that much more expensive.

What is the difference between Mexican oregano and Mediterranean oregano?

Mexican oregano is actually of the verbena family and not directly related to Greek or Italian oregano that is more commonly seen in most of the United States. Though not a true oregano, Mexican oregano is native to Mexico, Guatemala and parts of South America. It has a unique sweetness and intensity, but seems to be less pungent than other varieties of oregano. It is used dry because it lacks flavor when fresh.

What is epazote?

Epazote (ehp-ah-zoh-teh) is a classic seasoning for beans as it has an anti-flatulence quality. This pungent, annual herb grows wild in Mexico and the United States. Used dried or fresh, there is no substitute for its distinctive and incomparable flavor. It is also referred to as Mexican tea. It can be steeped in hot water and served to soothe an upset stomach.

Why should I purchase whole seeds (cumin and coriander) instead of ground?

We always recommend buying spices in their whole form. Nature created ingenious packaging systems for spices called seeds. Inside these seeds exist volatile compounds, which are what give spices their specific, aromatic signature. Once a spice has been removed from its seed and ground, the compounds volatilize and their quality quickly declines. We recommend toasting before grinding (see toasting spices p. 144).

Where do you store chile powders? For how long?

As with all aromatic ingredients, it is important to keep them in air-tight containers. The best place to store your air-tight container is in the freezer. The cooler the temperature, the longer your chile will be at its peak. The chile will not go bad if stored in the freezer, but after about six months, it will start to lose its punch. If you have had your chile powder in the freezer for longer than six months, you are not eating enough!

Which chile powder should I use to make red chile sauce?

Any red chile sauce served here in New Mexico is made with New Mexico red chile as the main ingredient. That doesn't mean other varieties of chile aren't used, but our famous red chile is always the place to start. The red chile can be referred to as Chimayo chile, chile molido or just New Mexico red chile.

Why do you use kosher salt rather than table salt?

Table salt, which is most commonly found in our homes, is mined and processed to form small, uniformly shaped cubes. Additives are used to prevent caking and some medical problems. Kosher salt is additive-free course-grained salt that we prefer because of its texture and flavor.

Is a tomatillo related to a tomato?

In most of Mexico, those pale green globes covered with a papery lantern shade husk, known to us as tomatillos, are called green tomatoes. However, this is misleading, as they are technically not green tomatoes. Tomatillos do not ripen to a red color and are only found green. They have a tangier, more citrusy flavor than a green tomato. Tomatillos are not botanically kin to the ordinary tomato, so do not substitute green tomatoes if tomatillos cannot be found.

Coffee grinders or spice mill: A $15 coffee grinder becomes a fantastic electric spice grinder. Your spices can be coarsely ground or reduced to a fine powder in this rather inexpensive tool. To keep your coffee from tasting like cumin, and to keep your cumin from tasting like coffee, clean the grinder by pulsing some dry rice and then wipe out the bowl with a dry paper towel; or better still, buy one for each purpose.

Santa Fe School of Cooking Grill: Although this device was originally designed for the sole purpose of roasting green chiles, we have found it to be very versatile. Try grilling red onion slices and pineapple for the body of a fantastic fruit salsa. Some of our chefs blacken tomatoes right on the stovetop grill to use in red chile sauce. We sell so many of these that we decided to start having them made for us! They work on gas, electric or ceramic-top ranges.

Citrus Squeezers: Available in lime, lemon and orange sizes (grapefruit is currently under development). These tools have become favorites at the SFSC. Not only are they easy to operate, they are able to extract every drop of juice from your citrus fruit. To ensure optimum juice yield from your fruit, first roll the whole fruits between your palm and work surface to soften. Then slice in half, place the fruit *peel side up* in squeezer and squeeze.

Zester: Some chefs use a pairing knife to carefully cut away the aromatic portion of the peel while others use vegetable peelers or fine cheese graters.

We recommend a combination grater/zester, which is a sharp stainless blade with non-clogging teeth. These hand-held gadgets remove only the colorful, flavorful part of the citrus peel, and leave the white, bitter pith behind. We recommend the Microplane brand of grater/zester, as it has a comfortable black handle to hold and a large grating surface.

Tortilla Basket: At the SFSC, we keep our tortillas warm in handmade baskets made by the Tarahumara Indians of northern Mexico. They are double-woven, beargrass baskets that have lids to fit. Not only is it practical, but wrapping the warm tortillas in a terrycloth towel inside the basket makes for a lovely presentation.

Micaceous pots: We recommend the La Chamba black clay pots from Colombia to make your soups, stews and beans, as well as enchiladas. Cooking in the clay dishes also adds subtle, earthy nuances that metal doesn't give. They also look great for serving, so a piece can go straight from the oven or stovetop to the table.

Tortilla press: This is used when making corn tortillas to press out and flatten the dough. We recommend a steel or aluminum press, as many of the presses on the market are of inferior quality and will break easily.

Suribachi: This is the Japanese version of a mortar and pestle. It has small ridges on the inside that are ideal for grinding herbs and spices as it keeps the ingredient in the bowl and gives a rough surface for cracking spices.

Aji Amarillo SALSA

CORNMEAL-CRUSTED GOAT CHEESE WITH HOT SALSA

MEATBALLS WITH SALSA ROMESCO

DUCK TAMALES

SMOKED CHILE MUSSELS

ACHIOTE CITRUS CHICKEN IN BANANA LEAF

Appetizers

ARGENTINE EMPANADAS
WITH AJI AMARILLO SALSA

YIELDS 20 EMPANADAS

PICADILLO FILLING:

1	tablespoon olive oil
½	cup finely diced onion
2	teaspoons minced garlic
½	pound lean ground beef or turkey
½	teaspoon toasted ground cumin seed
1	teaspoon ancho chile powder
2	teaspoons chile caribe
¼	teaspoon ground clove
½	cup raisins or currants, soaked in ½ cup Madeira wine
½	cup chopped pimiento-stuffed olives
½	cup toasted slivered almonds, chopped
3	hard-boiled eggs, peeled and chopped

Salt and pepper to taste

DOUGH

2	cups unbleached all-purpose flour
½	teaspoon salt
1½	cups (3 sticks) unsalted butter, cut into 12 pieces
6	ounces cream cheese, cut into tablespoon-sized pieces
1	egg plus 1 yolk whisked with ¼ cup water

These pastry turnovers were developed for our New World Tapas class by James Campbell Caruso of El Farol, Santa Fe's famous tapas restaurant. The pastry recipe works well with any filling, savory or sweet. These are great party fare because they can be filled and kept refrigerated or frozen until baking time.

FOR THE FILLING:

Heat the oil in a large skillet and sauté the onion and garlic until soft. Add the beef or turkey in small bits, breaking it up as it browns. Add the spices and raisins with their liquid and continue to cook until most of the liquid has evaporated. Stir in the remaining ingredients and season to taste with salt and pepper.

FOR THE DOUGH:

1. Preheat oven to 450° F.

2. Pulse the flour and salt in a food processor to blend. Add the butter and cream cheese and process until the dough comes together in a ball.

3. Remove the dough and place on a lightly floured surface. Roll dough to a thickness of about 1/8 inch. Cut circles of dough with a 3-inch cutter.

4. Brush the circles with egg wash and place about 2 teaspoons of filling in the center of each circle.

5. Fold the circles over the filling and crimp the edges with the tines of a fork.

6. Place the finished empanadas on a nonstick baking sheet and brush each with egg wash. Bake for about 8 to 10 minutes, until golden. Serve warm with Aji Amarillo Salsa.

(continued on page 36)

Aji Amarillo Salsa

YIELD: ABOUT 2 CUPS

3 or 4 aji amarillo pods, stems removed

2 cups water for soaking chiles

2 tablespoons roasted peanut oil

½ yellow onion, diced

4 cloves garlic, minced

2 Roma or yellow plum tomatoes, diced

2 teaspoons lime juice

Salt to taste

1. Soak the chile pods in warm water for 45 minutes. Drain and discard the water.

2. Pour 1 tablespoon peanut oil into a small saucepan over high heat. Sauté onion until soft and add the garlic. Add the tomatoes and sauté for 1 minute. Place onion, garlic and tomato mixture in a blender then add chile to blender and mix until pureed. Add the water. Place the remaining tablespoon oil in the saucepan and add back the chile puree and bring to a boil. Reduce the heat and simmer for about 10 minutes. Add the lime juice. Adjust the seasoning with salt. Thin with a little water, if needed.

This salsa is quite different from the New Mexican salsas we are more familiar with.

Look for a variation of this recipe in James Campbell Caruso's cookbook, *El Farol: Tapas and Spanish Cuisine* (Gibbs Smith, Publisher, 2004).

When you are in New Mexico and say the word *chile*, people automatically assume you are speaking of New Mexican chiles—red or green. However, when in South America, aji is the general term for chile peppers. Ajis are generally about an 8 on the heat scale of 1–10 and can rival some habaneros with their hot fruity flavor. The pods are yellow at some time during growth, giving rise to the common name Aji Amarillo, although there are other varieties of aji.

Spanish Tortilla

SERVES 8 TO 12 FOR TAPAS, 4 FOR SUPPER

⅓ cup plus 1 tablespoon fruity Spanish olive oil, divided

2 pounds baking potatoes, peeled and thinly sliced

1 large onion, peeled and thinly slivered or diced

Salt and freshly ground black pepper

6 large eggs, lightly beaten

4 tablespoons chopped Italian flat-leaf parsley, divided

Our two tapas classes are some of the most popular ones we offer. Tapas are traditionally known as "the little dishes of Spain." Most of our tapas here have a Southwestern twist added; however, this tapa remains unchanged from its original form. Potato omelet, or Tortilla Espanola, is the all-time tapas classic and is served in all tapas bars in Spain. Not only can it be made in advance, but it also tastes better and is easier to cut when served at room temperature.

1. Preheat the broiler.

2. Heat 1/3 cup olive oil in a wide nonstick or cast-iron skillet. Add the potatoes and cook over medium heat, stirring frequently, until they are cooked through and golden, about 20 minutes. Separate any slices that stick together so they cook evenly. Using a slotted spoon, transfer the potatoes to a plate with a slotted spoon. Add remaining oil and sauté the onion until lightly browned. Add onion to the potatoes and season with salt and pepper.

3. Return the potatoes and onion to the skillet over medium heat, and pour in the eggs. Sprinkle with 2 tablespoons parsley and smooth down any potatoes and onions that stick up. Cook over low heat until golden on the bottom, about 8 minutes.

4. Slip the skillet under the broiler and cook the tortilla until just set, about 5 minutes. Remove from heat and turn out onto a serving platter. Cut into wedges or squares and sprinkle with remaining parsley. Serve slightly warm or at room temperature. We like to serve this with Salsa Romesco (see page 52).

At the Santa Fe School of Cooking, we primarily use Italian flat-leaf parsley. It has a fresh, slightly peppery flavor that is stronger than the curly leaf parsley that is easier to come by. However, if you can't find Italian flat-leaf parsley, it is fine to use curly leaf.

SHRIMP CEVICHE

SERVES 14

2 pounds frozen shrimp
    (16/20 size), thawed,
    peeled and deveined
Olive oil
1 medium white onion,
    finely chopped
1 cup chile sauce or
    tomato ketchup
¼ cup chopped fresh
    parsley
¼ cup chopped fresh
    cilantro
½ cup pimiento-stuffed
    green olives, chopped
Pickled serrano or jalapeño
    chiles, to taste, chopped
Juice from the can of pickled
    chiles to taste
2 tablespoons
    Worcestershire sauce
1 teaspoon dried Mexican
    oregano
Juice of 2 fresh oranges
Juice of 2 fresh limes
Salt to taste

1. Split the shrimp in half lengthwise and set aside.

2. Heat the oil in a large sauté pan over high heat. Sauté the shrimp in batches until just cooked. Set aside to cool.

3. Place the remaining ingredients in a large bowl and mix well. Salt to taste, and then stir in the shrimp. Flavors and textures are at their peak within 3 hours of making this dish, so plan accordingly. Serve with a wedge of lime and soda crackers.

Achiote Citrus Chicken in Banana Leaf

SERVES 8

Juice of 4 oranges

Juice of 2 limes

2   tablespoons achiote paste

4   cloves garlic, minced

1   tablespoon salt

4   (4-ounce) chicken breasts, boneless, skinless and cut in half

8   pieces of banana leaf, cut in 4-inch squares and 8 strips for tying

These little delicacies are great because they are so easy to make and yet look elegant when served. The banana leaf can be hard to find. Try looking at Asian specialty shops. If you can't find them, you can use corn husks instead.

1. Combine fruit juices with the achiote paste, garlic and salt, and mix well. Toss with the chicken pieces and marinate for 1 hour.

2. Place a chicken piece in the center of each banana leaf and drizzle with marinade. To close the leaf, fold in the sides and then the top and bottom. Wrap a strip around once and tie.

3. Heat a grill to medium. Grill chicken bundles 4 minutes on each side. The chicken will steam in its juices.

Recipe contributed by James Campbell Caruso. A version of this recipe may be found in his book, *El Farol: Tapas and Spanish Cuisine.*

The annatto seed, called achiote in Mexico, is used for color and flavor, most commonly in regional Mexican dishes from the southern and southeastern parts of the country. A small tree, native of tropical America, produces a brown, rough-skinned, oval husk, the inside of which is packed with very small seeds covered with a layer of matte red pigment. The seeds are very hard to find; it is more common to find achiote paste, in which the seeds are ground and mixed with vinegar, salt, garlic and spices.

Duck Tamales

YIELDS 24 TAMALES

MASA

6 tablespoons unsalted
butter, softened
1 teaspoon baking powder
1 teaspoon salt
2 cups masa harina
2 to 2½ cups warm water
(or as needed)

FILLING

1 bunch scallions, finely
chopped
4 duck legs
¾ cup dark soy sauce
1½ cups brown sugar
2 small oranges, cut in
half
3 tablespoons fresh
gingerroot, chopped
1 stick canela
2 pieces star anise
2 guajillo chiles
Water as needed

This masa recipe is slightly nontraditional, but the light, creamy texture is fantastic with the duck filling!

FOR THE MASA

1. Cream together butter, baking powder, salt and masa harina with an electric mixer until a light, even texture is achieved. With the motor running, pour in warm water until a creamy, spreadable texture is achieved. Cover tightly and set aside at room temperature until needed.

FOR THE FILLING

1. Reserving 1/2 cup chopped scallions, place all other ingredients in a stockpot and add water until legs are just covered. Bring mixture to a simmer and cook until meat pulls easily away from the bone (approximately 1 1/2 hours).

2. Remove legs and reserve liquid. Pick the meat and skin from the bone and place in the work bowl of an electric mixer.

3. Return bones to the liquid and simmer to reduce until a syrupy consistency is achieved. Strain liquid to use later on cooked tamales.

4. Add the reserved scallions to the meat and mix until it has the appearance of pulled pork.

5. Follow the Technique of Making Tamales on page 42.

6. Open each tamale husk and drizzle approximately 1 tablespoon of the syrupy duck sauce over the top.

TO SOFTEN CORN HUSKS

Soak in warm water overnight or immerse in boiling water for an hour. Drain.

TO ASSEMBLE

1. Place 1 to 2 tablespoons of prepared masa in the center of a softened corn husk and spread it into a rectangle.

2. Add several teaspoons of filling down the center of the masa.

3. Fold one side of the corn husk over the filling.

4. Fold the opposite side over the folded side.

5. Tie the ends of the tamale with a piece of the corn husk torn lengthwise like string, or, alternatively, fold both ends of the tamale up and secure with a strip of the husk, forming more of a rectangle.

TO COOK

1. Fill the bottom of a steamer with 2 to 3 inches of water and drop a pebble in the bottom. Place the basket in the steamer and line it with some extra corn husks. Place the tamales in flat layers on the corn husks and cover the tamales with a few more of the husks so they don't dry out.

2. Cover the steamer with its lid. Bring the water to a boil and cook the tamales for 45 to 50 minutes, or until they feel firm to the touch and the husk easily peels away from the masa.

3. Listen to the pot while it boils; the pebble will make a noise on the bottom of the pan. If the pan boils dry, you will not hear the noise—a signal to add more water. Let the tamales rest for 5 minutes and serve.

Blue Corn Tamales with Calabacitas (Squash) Filling

YIELDS 12 TAMALES

BLUE CORN MASA

½ cup blue cornmeal
½ cup tamale grind masa harina
½ teaspoon baking powder
½ teaspoon kosher salt
⅓ cup plus 1 tablespoon lard or vegetable shortening
½ to ¾ cup warm chicken broth or water

FILLING

2 tablespoons olive oil
½ cup chopped onion
2 teaspoons minced garlic
1 medium zucchini, diced (about 1 cup)
1 cup whole kernel corn
½ cup green chile, (can use a combination of half hot and half mild)
1 teaspoon Mexican oregano
½ cup grated Monterey Jack cheese
Salt and pepper to taste
3 ounces dried cornhusks, soaked in warm water overnight or immersed in boiling water for 1 hour and drained

FOR THE MASA

1. Place the blue cornmeal and masa harina, baking powder and salt in a bowl and whisk to combine.

2. Place the lard in the bowl of an electric mixer fitted with the paddle attachment. Beat until lard is white and fluffy.

3. Add the dry ingredients by the spoonful and beat on low to mix.

4. Slowly add the broth or water until everything is combined. Turn the mixing speed to high and beat for 10 to 12 minutes, until light and fluffy.

FOR THE FILLING

1. Heat the oil in a skillet over medium-high heat. Add the onion and cook, stirring, for 1 minute.

2. Add the garlic and the zucchini and cook, stirring frequently, for 2 to 3 minutes.

3. Add the corn, green chile and oregano and continue to heat through.

4. Remove mixture from the heat, place in a bowl, and let cool for 10 minutes. Stir in cheese and use salt and pepper to taste. Set aside.

Follow the Technique of Making Tamales on page 42.

Blue corn, which varies in color from light gray to almost black, is an ingredient that seems to be unique to New Mexico. The ground meal made from blue corn is nuttier in flavor, higher in protein, and lower in starch than the meal made from either white or yellow corn. The Native Americans cultivated blue corn hundreds of years ago for use in their ceremonies honoring the regeneration of Mother Earth.

Red Chile Hummus with Vegetable "Chips"

YIELDS 2 TO 2½ CUPS

2½ cups cooked chickpeas
½   cup tahini
6   cloves garlic, peeled
3   tablespoons fresh lemon
    juice
1   tablespoon Chimayo
    chile powder
¼   cup cold water
Salt and pepper to taste
1   tablespoon olive oil
Variety of thinly sliced
    vegetables such as
    cucumber, tomato, bell
    pepper and zucchini

This recipe is one of our recent additions for our low-carb Southwest class. You can't always find good hummus in the stores, but it is so easy to make! We serve this with raw vegetables, but hummus is traditionally served with pita bread.

1. Combine all ingredients except olive oil and sliced vegetables in food processor and process until smooth. With motor running, slowly drizzle in olive oil. Serve with vegetable "chips," such as sliced cucumber, tomato, bell pepper and zucchini.

Achiote Tamales with Shrimp

YIELDS 12 TAMALES

ACHIOTE MASA

1   cup tamale grind masa harina
½   teaspoon baking powder
¾   teaspoon kosher salt
⅓   cup plus 1 tablespoon lard or vegetable shortening
1   ounce (1 block) achiote condimentado, grated or crumbled
¾   to 1 cup chicken broth

FILLING

2   tablespoons olive oil
¼   cup chopped onion
1   teaspoon minced garlic
12 to 14 ounces shrimp, peeled, deveined and coarsely chopped
2   ripe Roma tomatoes, roasted and diced
¼   teaspoon Mexican oregano
1   tablespoon chopped fresh epazote or 2 tablespoons dried
1   tablespoon chopped fresh cilantro
Kosher salt and freshly ground black pepper to taste
12 pieces of banana leaf, cut in 4-inch squares and 12 strips for tying

FOR THE MASA

1. Place masa harina, baking powder and salt in a bowl and whisk to combine.

2. Place lard in the bowl of an electric mixer fitted with the paddle attachment. Beat until the lard is white and fluffy.

3. Add the dry ingredients and achiote by the spoonful and beat on low to mix.

4. Slowly add the broth until everything is combined. Turn the mixing speed to high and beat for 10 to 12 minutes, until light and fluffy.

FOR THE FILLING

1. Heat the oil in a skillet over medium-high heat. Add onion and cook, stirring for 1 minute.

2. Add garlic and shrimp and cook for 1 minute more.

3. Add tomatoes and cook for 2 minutes, or until the mixture has dried out slightly.

4. Add oregano, epazote and cilantro and season to taste with salt and pepper. Stir to combine well and set aside to cool.

Follow the Technique of Making Tamales on page 42 using either banana leaves or softened corn husks. If using banana leaves, fold in the sides around the filling, then fold the top and bottom. Wrap a strip around once and tie.

CORNMEAL-CRUSTED GOAT CHEESE WITH HOT TOMATO SALSA

SERVES 6

2 eggs
1 cup milk
2 cups coarse cornmeal
1 tablespoon cracked black peppercorns
1 cup flour
9 ounces soft goat cheese
1 tablespoon roasted, peeled and diced green chile or pureed chipotles en adobo
2 cups vegetable oil

1. Whip eggs and milk together.

2. Mix cornmeal and peppercorns together.

3. Place flour on a piece of wax paper.

4. Combine goat cheese and chile; then divide the mixture into six equal parts. Roll into balls, and flatten at opposite ends for stability.

5. Dredge the goat cheese mixture in flour, followed by the egg wash and ending with the cornmeal mixture, being careful to coat the cheese completely.

6. Heat oil in a skillet over medium-high heat to 375° F and fry the cheese until golden brown. Remove the cheese with a slotted spoon and place on paper towels. Serve with Hot Tomato Salsa.

Hot Tomato Salsa

2 tablespoons olive oil
1 medium onion, finely diced
2 cloves minced garlic
2 teaspoons cumin seed, toasted and ground (see toasting spices p. 144)
4 medium tomatoes, diced
Salt to taste

1. Heat oil in a saucepan. Sauté onion until golden, adding the garlic during the last minute. Add the cumin, tomatoes and salt and simmer about 5 minutes, or until flavors come together.

SMOKED CHILE MUSSELS

SERVES 4 TO 6

3 tablespoons olive oil

Salt and freshly ground black pepper to taste

1 poblano or New Mexico green chile, seeded and diced

1 red bell pepper, seeded and diced

½ cup diced white onion

2 to 3 tablespoons garlic, coarsely minced

1 tablespoon chipotle seasoning

1 to 2 tablespoons smoked paprika (mild or hot)

½ teaspoon ground cumin

3 to 3½ pounds black or green lipped mussels, rinsed and de-bearded

2 to 3 tablespoons capers (optional)

2 ounces Pernod or Ouzo

2 cups dry but fruity white wine

¾ cup fish or chicken stock or water

4 ounces small cherry or pear tomatoes, halved (about 10 tomatoes)

Juice of ½ lemon or lime

⅓ cup chopped cilantro

5 tablespoons butter, cut in small pieces

Eddie Lyons gave us this recipe that was a favorite dish on his menu when he was the chef at The Galisteo Inn. It was inspired from the mussels he used to eat at the beach everyday when he was staying in San Sebastian, Spain.

1. Preheat a large skillet or saucepan over high heat. Add oil, season with salt and pepper and add the diced chiles, pepper and onion. Sauté until color begins to develop, add the garlic and cook until slightly browned.

2. Add the chipotle seasoning, paprika and cumin, stir briefly and add the mussels and optional capers.

3. Stir well and sauté for about 1 minute then deglaze with the Pernod followed by the wine (be careful, as the alcohol may flame).

4. After the flames subside, add the stock or water, tomatoes, and the lemon juice, cover and steam over high heat until the mussels open (about 4 to 5 minutes).

5. Add the cilantro and the butter and mix well over the heat until all of the butter is incorporated. Discard any unopened mussels, adjust the seasonings and serve.

When shopping for mussels, you need to look for tightly closed shells; otherwise the mussels are not fresh and alive. Shucked mussels should be plump, with their liquid clear. Smaller mussels will be more tender than larger ones. Fresh mussels, live or shucked, should be stored in the refrigerator and used within a day or two.

CRAB & CORN FRITTERS
WITH RED CHILE GLAZE

SERVES 6 TO 8

¾ cup flour
2 teaspoons baking powder
1½ teaspoons salt
1½ tablespoons Chimayo chile powder
3 large eggs, lightly beaten
1 tablespoon sour cream
½ cup corn kernels
1 cup (packed) fresh crabmeat (picked over to remove any shell fragments)
Canola oil

Fritters will be different shapes and sizes and will therefore cook at different rates. Try timing one or two different sizes to find out what works best for you. Fritters should be seasoned with salt immediately after coming out of the oil and enjoyed as soon as they are ready.

1. Combine flour, baking powder, salt and chile powder in a mixing bowl. Add eggs and sour cream; whisk together until smooth. Add corn and crabmeat and combine.

2. Heat oil 3/4 inch deep in a heavy-bottomed pan over medium heat to 350° F. Carefully drop heaping tablespoon-sized dollops into hot oil. Cook for 4 to 5 minutes, or until golden brown on the outside and cooked through. Remove from oil with a slotted spoon and place on a paper towel–lined plate to drain off excess oil.

3. Serve with Red Chile Glaze.

RED CHILE GLAZE

2 cups apple cider vinegar
2 cups apple cider
1½ cups dark brown sugar
2 tablespoons chile caribe
1 stick canela

Combine all ingredients in a saucepan and place over medium-high heat. Simmer until reduced by approximately 75 percent, or until a syrupy consistency is achieved. Cool to room temperature before serving.

Meatballs with Salsa Romesco

SERVES 6

3 tablespoons bread crumbs

2 tablespoons chicken broth

1 pound ground beef, crumbled, (preferably not a lean cut, as fat keeps the meatballs moist)

2 cloves garlic, minced

1 tablespoon finely chopped fresh parsley

1 tablespoon finely chopped fresh mint or 1 teaspoon dried

1 teaspoon dried Mexican oregano

1 tablespoon grated Manchego or Parmesan cheese

1 egg, lightly beaten

This is another dish from our Southwest Tapas class. Salsa Romesco is a classic sauce from Catalonia, Spain. It is an extremely versatile condiment that you will use on everything! We like it with the Spanish Tortilla. This works great for parties. Salsa Romesco can be made ahead, as can the meatballs through step 2. Be sure not to over-cook the meatballs or they will dry out.

1. Preheat the oven to 350° F.

2. In a small bowl, soften the bread crumbs with the chicken broth for several minutes.

3. In a larger bowl, thoroughly mix the beef, softened crumbs and remaining ingredients. Shape the mixture into 1 1/2-inch balls and set aside. Heat a large skillet over medium-high and brown the meatballs in batches. As they brown, transfer them to a baking pan.

4. Finish meatballs in the oven for 10 to 12 minutes, until they are cooked through but not dry. Serve warm with Salsa Romesco.

Salsa Romesco

1 slice country-style French or Italian bread

Olive oil for frying

1/3 cup toasted almonds

1/3 cup toasted hazelnuts

3 cloves garlic

2 teaspoons chile caribe

4 Roma tomatoes

2 small red bell peppers, roasted, peeled and seeded

1 dried ancho chile or New Mexico dried red chile

Salt and pepper to taste

Sherry vinegar to taste

1/2 cup (more or less) extra virgin olive oil

1. Fry the bread in a little oil until crisp and golden. Cool.

2. In a food processor, process the bread, nuts, garlic and chile to fine crumbs. Add remaining ingredients, except vinegar and oil, and process until smooth. With the machine running, gradually add the vinegar and oil. Taste and adjust seasonings. Cover and let the salsa rest for 15 to 20 minutes.

STUFFED SQUASH BLOSSOMS WITH FRESH TOMATO SAUCE

SERVES 6

18 medium-sized squash blossoms, stamens removed

FILLING

4 ounces soft goat cheese

8 ounces ricotta cheese

1 tablespoon each chopped fresh cilantro and chives

Zest of 1 lemon

Sea salt and freshly ground pepper to taste

FRESH TOMATO SAUCE

4 medium-sized ripe tomatoes, stems removed

1 tablespoon extra virgin olive oil

½ teaspoon minced garlic

Sea salt and freshly ground black pepper to taste

BATTER

1 egg, lightly beaten

1½ cups ice water

1 cup unbleached all-purpose flour

Vegetable oil

Squash blossoms are available at the Santa Fe Farmers Market during the summer months. When we have Farmers Market classes, the class visits the market and helps buy the ingredients. The chefs always gravitate to squash blossoms for part of the meal. Also at the market, you can easily find wonderful fresh goat cheese from Sweetwoods Dairy, local heirloom tomatoes and an abundance of fresh herbs and garlic. What a treat!

Gently remove the center stamens from the blossoms. Give the blossoms a little shake to remove any insects or bits of dirt.

FOR THE FILLING

1. Combine the cheeses in a medium bowl. Stir in the herbs and lemon zest and season to taste with salt and pepper.

2. Place the filling in a pastry bag fitted with a 1/4-inch round tip, or use a small spoon, and fill each blossom with about 1 tablespoon of the cheese mixture. Arrange filled blossoms on a sheet pan lined with paper towels, cover with plastic wrap and chill for at least 45 minutes to firm up the filling.

FOR THE FRESH TOMATO SAUCE

1. Slice each tomato in half widthwise. Take one of the halves in the palm of your hand and grate the tomato flesh from its skin on the large holes of a box grater set in a bowl. Continue to grate remaining tomatoes. You should have about 1 1/2 cups of grated ripe tomato.

2. Heat the oil in a small skillet over medium heat. Add the garlic and sauté until very lightly golden. Immediately pour the garlic and oil into the grated tomato and stir to combine. Season with salt and pepper. Set aside.

FOR THE BATTER

1. Add the egg to the ice water and stir. Place the flour in a medium bowl and slowly stir in the ice water mixture. Don't worry if the mixture is lumpy.

2. Heat an inch of oil in a medium skillet over medium-high heat to about 375° F. Coat three of the blossoms in the batter and gently place them in the hot oil and quickly fry on both sides until golden. Move the blossoms to a sheet pan lined wih paper towels and continue frying remaining blossoms. Keep the fried blossoms in a preheated 200° F oven so they stay warm. Serve immediately with the Fresh Tomato Sauce.

Place about 1/4 cup of the sauce on individual plates and arrange three blossoms over top. Serve.

TORTILLA SOUP WITH CRISPY TORTILLA STRIPS

CORN CHOWDER WITH GREEN CHILE CROUTONS

WILD GREENS AND APPLE SALAD

RED PEPPER DRIZZLE

SANTA FE SUNSET SOUP

JICAMA AND CARROT SLAW

ROASTED RED PEPPER, CORN & ORZO SALAD WITH SHRIMP

SOUPS AND SALADS

Mushroom Soup

SERVES 8 TO 10

½ **ounce dried porcini mushrooms**

½ **ounce dried chanterelle mushrooms**

½ **ounce dried morel mushrooms**

4 **tablespoons extra virgin olive oil**

1 **large white onion, cut into slivers**

3 **cloves garlic, peeled and thinly sliced**

1¼ **pounds fresh mushrooms, wiped clean, trimmed and thinly sliced**

12 **sprigs epazote, or 2 tablespoons dried**

2 **sprigs fresh thyme**

2 **sprigs fresh oregano**

1 **sprig fresh rosemary**

3 **or 4 chiles de arbol, lightly fried**

2 **quarts chicken broth (or combination of chicken and beef broth)**

Salt to taste

Lime wedges and/or fresh epazote for garnish

1. Soak the dried mushrooms in hot water for 20 minutes. Drain and reserve. If the mushrooms are in very large pieces, cut them in half.

2. In a deep soup pot, heat the oil over medium-high heat, add the onion and sauté 3 minutes. Add the garlic and continue cooking for 5 minutes more. Add the fresh mushrooms and sauté until softened and lightly browned, about 5 minutes.

3. Add the drained, dried mushrooms. Tie the epazote, thyme, oregano and rosemary sprigs in a bundle with kitchen string and add to the pot. Add the chiles and the broth. Stir and bring to a boil. Reduce heat and simmer for about 1 hour.

4. Remove the herb bundle and salt to taste. Garnish with lime wedges or fresh epazote.

Tortilla Soup with Crispy Tortilla Strips & Avocado Relish

SERVES 6

1   **medium white onion, peeled and sliced in ¼-inch slices**

8   **ripe Roma tomatoes, halved**

6   **whole cloves garlic, peeled**

2   **guajillo chiles, stems, seeds and ribs removed**

2   **ancho chiles, stems, seeds and ribs removed**

12   **white or yellow corn tortillas**

2   **cups canola oil (for frying)**

6   **cups chicken stock**

1   **teaspoon Mexican oregano**

Kosher salt to taste

1. Preheat the broiler and place an oven rack in the top position. Cover a baking sheet with foil and brush with oil. Arrange onion slices and tomato halves on the sheet. Broil vegetables for 10 minutes. Add garlic cloves to the vegetables and continue to broil for 10 minutes more, until vegetables are lightly charred, rotating the pan to char evenly. Cool.

2. Heat a skillet over medium heat and toast the chiles, pressing down on them with a kitchen towel or the back of a large spoon, for a few seconds on each side. Transfer the toasted chiles to a saucepan, cover with hot water and place on a burner over low heat, covered. Let the chiles steep for 15 minutes or so, to completely reconstitute and soften.

3. In the meantime, cut 8 of the tortillas in quarters. Cut the remaining tortillas in half, then cut the halves into 1/4-inch strips. Heat the oil in a medium skillet or a large saucepan over medium-high heat (365 to 375 ° F). Fry tortilla quarters in several batches, turning them, until crisp and golden. Drain on paper towels. Fry tortilla strips in the same manner, separating them from the quarters. Place the tortilla quarters in a plastic bag and crush them finely with a rolling pin.

4. Drain the chiles, and place them in a blender along with the charred vegetables. Puree the mixture until smooth. Place the puree and chicken stock in a medium saucepan and bring to a boil, stirring occasionally. Add the crushed tortillas and oregano; season with salt, to taste. Simmer, uncovered, until the tortillas have softened and the soup has thickened slightly, about 30 minutes. Taste and adjust seasoning.

Avocado Relish

1 medium-ripe avocado, cut in ¼-inch dice

1 small ripe tomato, cut in ¼-inch dice

1 small white or red onion, finely diced

1 to 2 jalapeño chiles, stems and seeds removed, finely diced

2 tablespoons chopped fresh cilantro

2 teaspoons fresh lime juice

Kosher salt to taste

Cilantro sprigs and lime slices for garnish

1. Place all ingredients except garnish in a small bowl and gently stir until well combined.

2. Divide the soup among 6 soup bowls. Place a heaping tablespoon of the avocado relish in the center of each bowl and add fried tortilla strips over that. Garnish with cilantro and lime.

Corn Chowder with Green Chile Croutons

SERVES 6

6 large ears sweet corn or 6 cups frozen corn, thawed

5 tablespoons unsalted butter, divided

1 small white onion, finely chopped

3 cloves garlic

3 cups milk, plus more if needed

½ cup crème fraîche or heavy cream

Kosher salt to taste

1. Husk corn and remove the silk. Cut the kernels from cobs with a sharp knife or a mandoline. Transfer kernels to a blender. You should have about 4 cups of corn. If using defrosted frozen corn, simply place it in the blender.

2. Heat half the butter in a small skillet over medium heat. Add the onion and sauté until softened, about 5 minutes. Scrape onion into the blender and return the skillet to the heat. Melt 1 tablespoon butter in the skillet and add the garlic, sautéing until golden. Scrape contents of the skillet into the blender. Add 1 cup milk and process until smooth, adding a little more milk, if needed.

3. Melt the remaining butter in a large saucepan and add the puree. Add the remaining milk, partially cover and simmer 15 to 20 minutes over low heat, stirring frequently. Remove pan from the heat and strain soup through a medium mesh sieve. Return strained soup to low heat and whisk in the crème fraîche. To serve, garnish each portion with a few Green Chile Croutons.

Tip from Nicole: I was cutting corn off a cob in front of one of my uncles and he looked at me like I was crazy! "What are you doing?" I guess he had never thought that you could have fresh corn cut off the cob. When corn is in season there is nothing else like it! To get the corn off the cob, hold the ear with one end on the cutting board and carefully slice right down the ear on each side with a sharp knife. One ear of corn yields about 2/3 cup fresh kernels.

Green Chile Croutons

French baguette or rustic Italian bread cut into ½-inch cubes, about 1 cup

3 tablespoons olive oil

Kosher salt

1 tablespoon green chile dip mix or green chile powder

Preheat the oven to 400° F. Place the bread cubes in a bowl, drizzle with oil and sprinkle with salt. Spread the seasoned croutons on a baking sheet and toast in the oven for 7 to 10 minutes. Remove from the oven, return to the bowl and toss croutons with the green chile dip mix or green chile powder to coat.

Santa Fe Sunset Soup with Red Pepper Drizzle

A creation of Rocky Durham, this dish is a combination of two soups, Black Bean Soup and Sweet Corn Bisque, and it always gets rave reviews. Serve both soups in one bowl for fantastic color and flavor contrasts. To effectively create the two-soups-in-one-bowl effect, the soups must be of the same consistency. Try pouring them simultaneously from two pitchers into the bowl. These soups mingle to create one great appetizer or a hearty cool-weather lunch. They can also be enjoyed individually.

Black Bean Soup

YIELDS ABOUT 8 CUPS

2	tablespoons olive oil
2	cups chopped red onion
½	cup peeled, diced carrot
½	cup diced celery
4	slices bacon, chopped (optional)
4	cloves garlic, minced
1	tablespoon toasted, ground cumin seeds
1	tablespoon toasted, ground coriander seeds
1	pound black beans, picked over for stones, soaked overnight, drained
8	cups vegetable or chicken stock
½	teaspoon chipotle seasoning
1	tablespoon dried epazote

Salt and black pepper

1. In a large saucepan, heat the oil over medium heat. Add the onion, carrot and celery and cook for 4 to 5 minutes, stirring occasionally. Add the bacon and garlic and cook another 4 to 5 minutes, stirring frequently. Add the remaining ingredients, bring to a simmer, reduce the heat to low and cover. Cook for 2 hours and then check the beans for tenderness. If they are starting to soften, add 2 teaspoons of salt and 1/2 teaspoon of black pepper, stir, and continue to simmer until the beans are completely softened.

2. Place 3 cups of the soup in a blender and puree until smooth. Return the puree to the soup. Taste and adjust seasonings with more salt, pepper and chipotle seasoning, if needed.

(continued on page 66)

Sweet Corn Bisque

YIELDS ABOUT 8 CUPS

1 tablespoon oil
1 cup diced yellow onion
¾ cup diced celery
2 cloves garlic, minced
1 cup New Mexico green chile, hot or medium, roasted, peeled, seeded and chopped
4 cups frozen corn kernels, thawed
2 baking potatoes, peeled and diced
5 cups vegetable or chicken stock
1 cup heavy cream
1½ teaspoons salt
½ teaspoon freshly ground black pepper (optional)
Pinch of sugar, if needed

1. Heat the oil in a large saucepan over medium-high heat. Add onion and celery and cook for 2 minutes, stirring occasionally. Add the garlic and cook for 1 minute more, stirring once. Add the remaining ingredients, reduce the heat to medium and simmer for about 45 minutes, or until the potatoes are tender.

2. Place 3 cups of the mixture in a blender and puree until smooth. Return the puree to the soup and taste; adjust seasonings.

Red Pepper Drizzle

2 red bell peppers, roasted, peeled and seeded
6 cloves roasted garlic
2 tablespoons hot sauce, preferably Coyote Café's Howlin' Hot Sauce
1 teaspoon fresh thyme
1 cup extra virgin olive oil
Salt and pepper to taste

1. Combine the bell peppers, garlic, hot sauce and thyme in a blender. With the motor running, slowly pour in the oil. Adjust the seasoning with salt and pepper. Store the mixture in a squeeze bottle for later use.

Sprout & Endive Salad with Walnut Vinaigrette

SERVES 4

2 cups mixed sprouts (sunflower, radish, broccoli, alfalfa)

2 large Belgian endives, trimmed and cut in thin slivers on the diagonal

2 tablespoons snipped fresh chives

⅓ cup flat-leaf parsley leaves

FOR SALAD

1. Trim the root ends of the packaged sprouts. In a medium bowl, combine sprouts, endive, chives and parsley. Toss to combine thoroughly.

2. Serve with Walnut Vinaigrette. Add enough of the vinaigrette to lightly coat the vegetables. Adjust seasonings.

Walnut Vinaigrette

4 tablespoons sherry vinegar to taste

1 large shallot, peeled and finely chopped

Pinch of sugar

4 tablespoons canolive oil

4 tablespoons walnut oil

Kosher salt and freshly ground black pepper

1. Whisk all ingredients together in a small bowl. Taste and adjust seasonings.

Nopales & Golden Beet Salad

4   medium-sized golden (or red) beets

1   tablespoon white wine vinegar

2   tablespoons lime-, lemon- or orange-flavored olive oil

Kosher salt and freshly ground black pepper to taste

1½ pounds fresh nopal cactus paddles

2   or 3 tablespoons olive oil

1   small red onion, cut into slivers

For the best flavor, choose small- to medium-sized beets that are firm. Just before cooking, wash beets gently so as not to pierce the skin, which would result in the loss of color and nutrients. Peel the beets after they are cooked and cooled. The skin comes off very easily.

1. Place the beets in a small saucepan and cover with water. Bring to a boil and cook over medium heat until tender, about 45 to 60 minutes. Remove pan from the heat and let stand 15 minutes. Drain, peel and cut beets into thin wedges while still warm. Dress lightly with white wine vinegar and flavored oil; sprinkle with salt and pepper. Set aside.

2. Preheat oven to 450° F. Place oven racks at the middle and highest positions.

3. See Technique of Preparing Nopales (page 70).

4. Toss the cactus strips with the oil, salt and pepper, and place them on two foil-lined baking sheets in even layers. With one tray on each rack, roast for 20 to 25 minutes, switching the trays halfway through, until the edges of the strips are crisp and the color is drab green. The strips will have shrunken slightly and will be dry.

5. In a medium bowl, combine the nopal strips, beets and red onion. Drizzle with Marjoram Vinaigrette and let stand for 15 minutes to combine flavors. Serve at room temperature or chilled.

Nopales, or fresh cactus, is the fleshy, paddle-shaped stem of the prickly pear cactus. All varieties of prickly pear are edible, but it is best to look for a medium-sized variety that is relatively spine-less (this is probably what you would get in the United States anyway). What we see growing in the south-western part of the United States are generally thick-skinned, low-growing varieties that are not particularly tasty. Nopales are very common in Mexico and are beginning to have more of a presence in the States, as they are very healthy.

Marjoram Vinaigrette

2   tablespoons white wine vinegar

4   tablespoons lime-, lemon- or orange-flavored olive oil

2   shallots, minced

1   tablespoon fresh marjoram leaves, coarsely chopped

1   to 2 serrano chiles, minced

Sugar to taste (optional)

Thoroughly combine ingredients. Taste and adjust seasonings.

TECHNIQUE OF PREPARING NOPALES

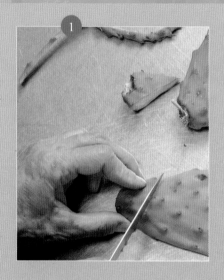

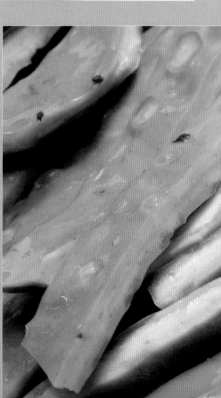

1. Lay the nopal paddle on a flat surface. With a sharp knife, trim the base of the paddle.

2. Trim around the outside edge of the paddle with the tip of the knife.

3. Carefully slice the thorny nods from the trimmed nopal paddle.

4. Clean nopal cactus paddle in water.

5. Cut the cleaned cactus paddle into 1/2-inch slices, widthwise, or diagonally across the paddle.

Wild Greens & Apple Salad

SERVES 10

1½ **pounds mixed wild**
   salad greens, washed
   and dried

1 **large red apple, cored**
   and thinly sliced

1 **large yellow apple,**
   cored and thinly sliced

⅓ **cup piñon nuts, lightly**
   toasted

1. Toss the wild greens with the Apple and Piñon Nut Dressing, and mound on ten salad plates. Arrange apple slices on greens and sprinkle with toasted piñon nuts.

Apple & Piñon Nut Dressing

⅓ **cup piñon nuts**

2 **teaspoons piloncillo**

2½ **teaspoons freshly**
   squeezed lime juice

4 **tablespoons apple juice**

6½ **tablespoons apple cider**
   vinegar

1½ **teaspoons toasted**
   poppy seeds

⅔ **cup canolive oil**

Salt and freshly ground
   pepper

1. Toast the piñon nuts in a small skillet until lightly browned, and then grind in a food processor and set aside. In the same skillet, heat the piloncillo and lime juice until caramelized. Stir in the apple juice and set aside to cool.

2. When cool, pour into a small bowl, add the vinegar, poppy seeds and ground piñon nuts and blend well. Slowly whisk in the oil; and add salt and pepper to taste.

Piloncillo are the cones of unrefined brown sugar from Mexico. They can be difficult to find in the United States and dark brown sugar can be substituted, although the flavor is a little different. To use piloncillo, you can chop it with a serrated knife, grate it or cook it in a microwave for 1 to 2 minutes to soften it. It will last indefinitely if stored in a dry place and wrapped well.

Tomatoes & Avocado with Chile Vinaigrette

SERVES 6

1½ to 2 pounds ripe tomatoes

2 ripe Haas avocados, pitted, peeled and sliced lengthwise

2 tablespoons snipped fresh chives

12 large fresh opal basil or green basil leaves, finely shredded

VINAIGRETTE

2 cloves peeled garlic

3 large poblano chiles, roasted, peeled and seeded (see Roasting Chiles p. 25)

1 tablespoon cider, white wine or rice wine vinegar

Pinch of sugar

Kosher salt and freshly ground pepper to taste

½ cup grapeseed oil

¼ cup lime-flavored olive oil

This simple but delicious summer salad was contributed by Kathi Long, who recommends heirloom tomatoes for this recipe. A similar version of this recipe is in her book which she did for Williams-Sonoma, The Southwest, *as part of the New American Cooking series, Time Life Books, Weldon Owen Production, 2001.*

FOR THE SALAD

1. Depending on the size and shape, core and slice, halve, or quarter the tomatoes. Arrange tomato and avocado slices on individual salad plates, dividing evenly, and drizzle each serving with the vinaigrette, dividing evenly. Sprinkle with chives and basil and serve immediately.

FOR THE VINAIGRETTE

1. Toast the garlic cloves in a small, dry frying pan over medium heat, turning as necessary, until golden, about 8 minutes. Let cool.

2. In a blender, combine the garlic, chiles, vinegar, sugar, salt and pepper and puree until smooth. If the ingredients do not puree easily, add a little water, 1 tablespoon at a time, to ease the blending. With the motor running, slowly add as much of the oil as needed to emulsify the mixture. It should be the consistency of heavy cream. If the mixture is too thick, add a little water. Taste and adjust the seasonings and then set aside.

Jicama & Orange Salad with Red Chile Vinaigrette

SERVES 6

3   seedless oranges

½   small pineapple, peeled, cored and cut into 1-inch cubes

1   small jicama, peeled and cut into ¾-inch cubes

1   medium red onion, cut in slivers

Kosher salt to taste

⅓   cup chopped fresh cilantro

The combination of jicama and oranges makes one think of the famous salad served on Christmas Eve in Mexico, Ensalada de Noche Buena. That salad has more ingredients, such as pomegranate and beets, but this version is ideal to serve in the middle of winter, when most fruits and vegetables aren't at their peak but jicama and oranges are.

1. Using a zester, remove the zest from one orange and finely mince. Set aside for the Red Chile Vinaigrette. Cut the stem and blossom ends from all the oranges. Then, standing each orange on a cutting board and, working close to the flesh, cut away the rind and all the white pith. Cut the oranges into chunks.

2. Combine the oranges, pineapple, jicama and onion in a bowl. Toss with Red Chile Vinaigrette. Add salt to taste. Divide the salad among six small salad plates and sprinkle with cilantro.

Red Chile Vinaigrette

1   tablespoon pure ground Chimayo red chile

1   tablespoon red chile caribe

½   cup sugar

¼   cup water

¼   cup fresh lime juice to taste

Reserved orange zest

Kosher salt to taste

Canola oil (optional)

1. Combine the red chile, chile caribe, sugar and water in a small saucepan and bring to a boil. Continue simmering for 3 minutes. Remove from the heat and let cool for 5 minutes. Stir in the lime juice, reserved orange zest, salt to taste and oil, if using.

Southwestern Caesar Salad

SERVES 4

4   cups romaine lettuce, inner leaves only

2   Roma tomatoes, diced

½   cup Caesar Vinaigrette

Red Chile Croutons

¼   cup Parmesan shavings for garnish

Caesar salad really doesn't seem very Southwestern. It was invented in Tijuana, Mexico, by an Italian immigrant. We have Southwesternized it by adding Chimayo chile powder to the dressing and croutons.

1. In a large bowl, toss the lettuce, tomatoes, Caesar Vinaigrette and Red Chile Croutons. Divide the salad among four serving plates and sprinkle with Parmesan shavings.

Caesar Vinaigrette

YIELDS ABOUT 2¼ CUPS

2   tablespoons chopped roasted garlic

½   cup red wine vinegar

1   tablespoon anchovy paste or 2 whole anchovies, mashed

1   tablespoon Dijon mustard

¼   cup grated Parmesan cheese

1   teaspoon Chimayo red chile powder

1   teaspoon salt

1   teaspoon freshly ground black pepper

1¼ cups olive oil

1. In a small bowl, combine all ingredients except oil. Whisk in oil. Adjust seasonings to taste.

Red Chile Croutons

2   teaspoons ancho or Chimayo chile powder

Salt and freshly ground pepper to taste

8   slices French or Italian bread, ½ inch thick, cut into cubes

1. Preheat the oven to 350° F.

2. Mix chile powder, salt and pepper together in a plastic bag. Add bread cubes to bag and shake well to coat.

3. Place seasoned bread cubes on lightly oiled baking sheet and spray with vegetable oil. Bake 10 to 15 minutes, or until lightly browned.

ROASTED RED PEPPER, CORN & ORZO SALAD WITH SHRIMP

SERVES 8

DRESSING

- ⅓ cup vinegar (white wine, champagne, sherry or another specialty vinegar)
- ⅔ cup flavored olive oil (lemon, lime, blood orange or grapefruit)
- 1 serrano pepper, chopped, or ½ chopped jalapeño
- 1 tablespoon honey
- 1 teaspoon salt
- 2 tablespoons sour cream
- ¼ cup roughly chopped cilantro

SALAD

- 16 to 24 shrimp, peeled, deveined, halved and cooked in seasoned liquid
- 1 cup (more or less) orzo, cooked according to package directions
- 1 poblano pepper, roasted, peeled, seeded and diced
- 1 red bell pepper, roasted, peeled, seeded and diced
- 1 yellow (or another color) bell pepper, roasted, peeled, seeded and diced
- 1 cup roasted corn kernels (frozen or canned may be substituted)
- ½ cup sliced green onions (white and green parts)
- Juice of 1 lime
- 2 to 3 ripe Haas avocados
- Cilantro, for garnish
- Lime wedges, for garnish

The beauty of this salad is that its ingredients are very versatile. The shrimp can be omitted and crab or lobster substituted. Fresh diced tomatoes can be added and different herbs can be used. Quinoa can be substituted for the orzo to reduce the carbohydrates and add protein to the salad.

It makes a great summer salad entrée and is ideal for picnics as it can be prepared ahead of time and assembled at the last minute.

FOR THE DRESSING

1. Put all ingredients into a jar, cover and shake. Chill and shake again before using.

FOR THE SALAD

1. Lightly coat shrimp with dressing, reserving most of dressing for the salad.

2. Combine all salad ingredients except shrimp, avocados, cilantro, lime juice and lime wedges.

3. Pour the remaining dressing over the ingredients.

4. Halve the avocados, remove the pit and scoop the avocado from the skin. Place on a plate and sprinkle with lime juice. Season with salt.

5. Spoon a portion of the dressed salad over the avocado. Garnish with shrimp, cilantro and lime wedges.

Farmers Market

The soil in Santa Fe, nestled at 7,000 feet in the foothills of the Rocky Mountains, is more sand than dirt. Piñon trees and cacti dot the arid landscape. Dust storms are more common than a humid day, and the average annual rainfall of 14 inches barely makes a dent in the seemingly endless drought. Not ideal conditions, you'd think, for growing anything green, but one visit to the Santa Fe Farmers Market would quickly change your mind.

Held every Tuesday and Saturday during the summer, the market is filled with booths selling a bounty of vegetables and fruits of every color. On a day in early June, red and yellow cherries are abundant, as are green sugar snap peas and purple radicchio. As the summer progresses, red tomatoes, green chiles and bright yellow corn take center stage. Milling around the booths, visitors and locals sample the cherries; buy and consume still-warm breakfast burritos and blueberry muffins, and fill their cloth bags with organic lamb chops, fresh basil, lavender-infused hand lotion, morning glory flowers and nearly everything home-grown or made in between. There's as much conversation in the aisles as there is in the booths; if you've lived in Santa Fe for more than a couple of months, running into friends and acquaintances at the market is a given. Two young girls, wearing matching pink boas and cowboy hats and playing violins, provide musical accompaniment to the scene.

Many of the booths are staples: the sprout table, which sells sunflower sprouts, buckwheat, pea shoot and daikon radishes, consistently has a line of locals next to it; the Sweetwood's goat cheese booth, where mouth-watering samples are generous, always draws a crowd (Haley, the daughter of school manager Nicole, loves stopping by it); a flatbed truck, owned by Jake West and full of his delicious namesake Jake melons, plus Schwebach corn from Moriarty. Many of these farmers travel 200 miles to bring their food to the market.

In addition to holding a special farmers market class in mid-August, during which students and a chef visit the market to scout out and buy the best ingredients, to create an impromptu meal, the school sells and uses products from a handful of vendors at the market. Having a chance to chat with them and see if they've got anything new we'd like to use is a good reason to visit the market; but, to be honest, just walking around the booths—seeing old friends and stocking our own refrigerators with local, organic fruits and veggies—is itself enough of a draw.

Beet & Spinach Salad with Balsamic Vinaigrette

SERVES 6 TO 8

2 baby beets

1 pound red cabbage, thinly sliced

½ pound spinach leaves, washed, dried and thinly sliced

¼ cup green scallions, sliced

1. Preheat oven to 350° F. Wrap beets in foil, place in oven and cook about 45 minutes or until soft. Let cool. Peel beets and grate on cheese grater so as to create thin matchstick pieces.

2. Combine beets, cabbage, spinach and scallions in a large bowl and toss well.

3. When ready to serve, toss the salad with a desired amount of Balsamic Vinaigrette and serve immediately.

Balsamic Vinaigrette

YIELDS ABOUT 1 CUP

½ cup balsamic vinegar

1 tablespoon sugar

1 teaspoon salt

½ teaspoon freshly ground pepper

½ cup low-fat chicken broth

2 teaspoons minced garlic

2 teaspoons Dijon mustard

2 tablespoons frozen orange juice concentrate

1. Place all ingredients in a small glass jar and shake until well blended.

NOTE: This dressing keeps well, refrigerated, for up to a week.

White Bean & Smoked Chile Salad

SERVES 8

4   **cups cooked white beans**

1   **red onion, diced**

1   **yellow or red bell pepper, diced**

3   **to 4 teaspoons of pureed chipotle en adobo sauce**

¼   **cup cilantro, well chopped**

Juice of 1 lime

1   **tablespoon cider vinegar**

3   **tablespoons extra virgin olive oil**

Salt to taste

Beans are one of the oldest foods around and were one of the first wild plants to be domesticated. Although beans are one of our staple foods here in New Mexico, the beans typically seen in this area are pinto beans or Anasazi beans.

Rinse beans well and combine all ingredients. Serve at room temperature for peak flavor.

Jicama & Carrot Slaw

SERVES 6

1 small jicama, about 4 to 6 ounces, peeled and julienned
2 carrots, peeled and julienned
½ to ¾ of a small red cabbage, finely shredded
Several handfuls of sunflower or radish sprouts, root ends trimmed

Combine the jicama, carrots, cabbage and sprouts. Toss thoroughly to distribute the ingredients evenly. Toss with Lime Vinaigrette and serve immediately.

Lime Vinaigrette

1 tablespoon finely chopped shallot
1 teaspoon seeded and minced serrano chile
3 tablespoons white wine vinegar
2 tablespoons freshly squeezed lime juice
2 tablespoons sugar
Kosher salt to taste
Lime oil to taste

Whisk together the shallot, chile, vinegar, lime juice, sugar and salt. Whisk in the oil. Set aside to allow the flavors to blend. Taste and adjust the seasoning.

Jicama & Grapefruit Salad with Avocado

SERVES 6

1   medium jicama, about 1 pound, peeled and cut into matchsticks

2   bunches watercress, washed, with large stems removed

1   English (seedless) cucumber, cut into julienne strips about 2 inches long

4   jalapeño chiles, stemmed, seeded and thinly sliced lengthwise

3   Texas ruby grapefruit

2   small, ripe Haas avocados, peeled, seeded and cut into thin slices

3   to 4 tablespoons extra virgin olive oil

Sugar to taste

Salt to taste

1. In a large bowl, gently toss the jicama, watercress, cucumber and chiles. Refrigerate until ready to use.

2. Peel and cut two of the grapefruits into segments. Add the segments and the avocado to the jicama mixture and gently toss.

3. Squeeze the juice of the third grapefruit into a small bowl. Whisk in oil, and season with sugar and salt to taste. Drizzle dressing over jicama mixture and serve immediately.

CORN FLAN

TWICE-FRIED PLANTAINS

TUMBLEWEED OF SWEET POTATO

MARINATED PURPLE POTATOES

SPICY PINTO BEANS

CHEESE GRITS

CHIPOTLE DOUBLE-COOKED POTATOES

Side Dishes

SAVORY RICE PUDDING

SERVES 12 TO 14

This is served as a side dish at the school, but it could be served as a main entrée because it is so hearty and filling! This makes a great dish for entertaining, as it can be prepared ahead of time, refrigerated, and then baked the next day.

TOMATO SAUCE

¼   cup extra virgin olive oil
1   large white onion, peeled and cut into slivers
3   cloves garlic, minced
1   28-ounce can whole plum tomatoes in juice, coarsely pureed
1   15-ounce can diced tomatoes in juice
6   poblano chiles, roasted, peeled, seeded and cut into thin strips (see p. 25 for roasting instructions)
1   teaspoon dried Mexican oregano
2   bay leaves
Pinch of sugar
Salt and freshly ground pepper to taste

CREAM SAUCE

2   cups crème fraîche
2   cups plain yogurt
Salt and freshly ground pepper to taste

TO ASSEMBLE

1½   cups grated mozzarella cheese
1½   cups grated Monterey Jack cheese
6   cups cooked long grain white rice (2 cups raw)

FOR TOMATO SAUCE

1. Heat the oil in a medium saucepan. Sauté the onion and garlic until softened and slightly browned. Add tomatoes and chile strips and cook for another 5 minutes. Season with oregano, bay leaves, sugar, salt and pepper to taste. Simmer for 20 minutes, until slightly thickened.

FOR CREAM SAUCE

Stir crème fraîche and yogurt together. Season with salt and pepper.

TO ASSEMBLE

1. Preheat oven to 350° F. Butter a large (3-quart) baking dish.

2. Toss the mozzarella and Monterey Jack cheeses together in a bowl.

3. Spoon half the rice into the dish and smooth evenly. Cover with half the tomato sauce and then half the cream sauce. Spread half the cheese over the cream sauce. Repeat with the remaining rice, sauce, and cream. Reserve the remaining cheese. Lightly cover the casserole with foil and bake about 30 minutes, until heated through. Uncover and sprinkle with reserved cheese. Return the uncovered casserole to the oven and bake for 10 to 15 minutes more, or until cheese melts.

Saffron Rice

SERVES 6

2 tablespoons olive oil
1 cup basmati rice
4 bay leaves
¼ teaspoon saffron
1 teaspoon kosher salt
1½ cups plus 2 tablespoons chicken broth

1. Heat the oil in a 2-quart saucepan over medium heat. Add the rice, bay leaves, saffron, and salt, and stir until the grains are opaque, 3 to 4 minutes. Continue stirring until the grains begin to color a light tan, 2 to 3 minutes longer.

2. Add the chicken broth, stir well and bring to a boil. Cover the pan, reduce to low heat and simmer until the liquid has been absorbed and the rice is tender, 25 to 30 minutes. Uncover, stir the rice and recover the pot. Remove from the heat and let the rice "steam" for 5 minutes longer.

3. Fluff the rice with a fork, remove the bay leaves and discard. Serve.

SAFFRON VS. AZAFRAN
Saffron holds the title as the world's most expensive spice. Saffron is the yellow-orange stigma from a small purple crocus. Each flower provides only three stigmas, which must be hand picked and dried. It takes over 14,000 of these tiny stigmas for each ounce of saffron! You can find saffron powdered or as threads (stigmas). We recommend using the threads and crushing them right before use. Store your saffron in an airtight container in a cool, dark place, so your expensive spice doesn't go to waste! Here in New Mexico, the use of azafran, "poor man's saffron," is much more prevalent than saffron. Azafran is the orange-red stamens of safflower, but it doesn't impart the same flavor as saffron and is not recommended in place of it. Azafran is used for its subtle, aromatic flavor and adds a wonderful color to dishes.

Tumbleweed of Sweet Potato

SERVES 8

3   to 3½ pounds sweet
    potatoes or yams, peeled
    and cut into long
    matchsticks
2   tablespoons melted
    butter
1   teaspoon Santa Fe
    Seasons Sweet Spices or
    blend of cinnamon,
    allspice and cloves
1   teaspoon ancho chile
    powder
½   teaspoon ground black
    pepper
2   tablespoons brown sugar

When shopping for sweet potatoes, look for medium-sized firm ones, with skin even in color and free of blemishes. Do not store them in the refrigerator, unless cooked. Store them in a cool, dry place (between 55 and 60° F). For the best flavor, they should be used within a week of purchase.

1. Preheat oven to 350° F.

2. In a bowl, toss sweet potato sticks with melted butter. Combine remaining ingredients, add to sweet potatoes, and toss to thoroughly coat.

3. Place mixture in a baking dish and cover with foil. Bake for 20 minutes, and then uncover and bake for 25 minutes more, or until tender.

The sweet potato has been gaining in popularity lately as the South Beach and Atkins diet crazes have taken over millions of Americans. Both diets frown on the potato but encourage substituting sweet potatoes in the later phases of these diets, as they are ranked much lower than white potatoes in the glycemic index. The sweet potato is a complex carbohydrate that provides twice the recommended daily allowance of vitamin A and more than a third of the allowance for vitamin C.

Lemon Southwest Rice

SERVES 6 TO 8

2   tablespoons butter
1   cup leeks, white part only,
    cleaned and thinly sliced
1   tablespoon finely minced
    garlic
2   cups uncooked white rice
3½ cups chicken broth
½   cup lemon juice, freshly
    squeezed
2   teaspoons freshly grated
    lemon rind
1   teaspoon azafran
1   teaspoon toasted and
    ground coriander seeds*
1   teaspoon salt
White pepper to taste
½   cup green chiles, roasted,
    peeled and chopped
¼   cup finely minced cilantro

1. In a nonstick saucepan, heat the butter until sizzling and then sauté leeks over medium heat until softened. Add the garlic and sauté 1 minute, stirring often. Add the rice and stir to coat. Add the chicken broth, lemon juice, lemon rind, azafran, coriander, salt and pepper. Bring to a boil, cover and reduce heat. Simmer slowly for approximately 20 to 30 minutes. Remove pan from heat and allow rice to rest for 5 minutes.

2. Add the chiles and cilantro to the rice, stirring well to combine.

*See toasting spices p. 144.

Herb-Roasted Vegetables

SERVES 4 TO 6

¾ **pound small, new, yellow or red potatoes, unpeeled and halved**

Olive oil

1 **to 2 teaspoons fresh thyme leaves, chopped**

Sea salt and freshly ground black pepper to taste

1 **medium fennel bulb, stem trimmed**

2 **bell peppers (red and yellow) seeded and cut in 1-inch squares**

3 **large carrots, peeled and sliced ¼ inch thick on the diagonal**

1 **pound asparagus, trimmed into 6-inch lengths from the tips**

1 **medium zucchini or yellow summer squash, sliced ¼ inch thick**

The vegetables in this dish cook at different times. We recommend preparing the vegetables first and then setting the timer to remind you to add the vegetables at the appropriate times. The quantity of vegetables used will affect the time, so watch carefully to make sure the vegetables are cooking appropriately.

1. Preheat the oven to 350° F. Toss potato halves in 1 or 2 tablespoons oil and 1 teaspoon thyme leaves; sprinkle with salt and pepper. Place in a large baking sheet or dish so the vegetables can cook as a single layer; roast on the middle rack of the oven for about 15 minutes.

2. Prepare the fennel bulb by cutting it in half widthwise through the core. Cut each half in half through the core, and then cut the quarters in half, or, if they are large, cut them in three pieces through the core. Mix the fennel, peppers and carrots with oil, salt, pepper and a little more thyme, and add to the potatoes on the baking sheet. Continue cooking for another 15 minutes.

3. Toss the asparagus and squash in a little oil and sprinkle with salt and pepper. Add the asparagus and squash by gently placing them with the other vegetables in a single layer on the baking sheet. Continue cooking 15 minutes more, or until vegetables are cooked through.

4. Remove vegetables from oven and serve.

At the Santa Fe School of Cooking, we always recommend reading a recipe all the way through, and then assembling all the ingredients necessary and getting them ready to combine, up to the point of cooking. The French term for this process is *mise en place.*

Wildcrafting

Whether wildcrafting in the countryside or standing in nearly100-degree heat on a mid-May day on his farm, Lawrence Sanchez seems oblivious to the beating sun overhead. "Sometimes I don't eat lunch until three," the sixty-five-year-old says. "And I don't stop working until it's dark." Sanchez, a retired USDA county service director, is surveying his 11-acre farm that is near the banks of the Rio Grande and has been in his family for nearly half a century. Walking along impossibly neat rows, he points out where Mexican melons, blue corn and Joe Parker chiles, among other things, will soon sprout. Although Sanchez, a quick-witted man, is too modest to admit it, he's planted everything, minus the wild asparagus growing around the perimeter, with his own leathered hands, using only organic farming methods.

He ambles over to two rows of epazote, a pungent herb that flavors anti-nausea tea and removes flatulence from beans. Leaves no bigger than a ladybug are poking out of the ground. Anybody, save Sanchez, would miss them, but he quickly points out the beginnings of the crop that will sooner than later end up in tins in the market at the Santa Fe School of Cooking and in the pots for black bean soup during classes. He has honed his eyes through a life-time of scouting plants in the wild, continuing the centuries-old Hispanic tradition of *curanderos*, folk healers whose holistic treatment of ailments included aloe vera, chamomile and other native herbs. "My mom would just tell me or one of my ten siblings to go find something she needed for cooking or medicine, and we'd do it," says Sanchez, who doesn't consider himself a curandero, although he definitely possesses the requisite knowledge. As an adult, for more than twenty years Sanchez has scouted out at least 160 herbs and spices in nature for medicinal (and cooking) purposes and sold them to local pharmacies throughout the state.

Along with epazote, Sanchez supplies the school with juniper berries, Mexican oregano and a variety of other herbs essential to Southwestern cooking. He's just one of a handful of local farmers that, in labor-intensive ways, grow and process unique ingredients, like posole (lime-soaked corn kernels), atole (toasted blue corn meal) and, of course, a wide variety of chiles, and supplies them to the school. It's a win-win situation: their products contribute to the authentic New Mexican flavors of the school and its product line, and we, in turn, are helping to preserve—and share—the region's historic and distinctive culinary traditions.

Braised Swiss Chard

SERVES 8

3   tablespoons olive oil
3   cloves garlic, sliced
2   pounds Swiss chard, washed, drained, stems removed and cut into thirds
Juice of ½ lemon or lime
1   tablespoon red wine vinegar
1   teaspoon chile caribe
Salt and pepper to taste

1. Preheat skillet on high heat. Heat oil, then add garlic, immediately followed by chard. Sauté for 2 to 3 minutes, stirring often.

2. Add lemon or lime juice, vinegar and chile caribe and stir well. Remove from heat, season with salt and pepper, and cover for 1 minute. Serve immediately.

Couscous with Vegetables

SERVES 6

3   tablespoons olive oil
⅓   cup diced red onion
1   clove garlic, minced
⅓   cup diced carrot
⅓   cup diced red bell pepper
⅓   cup diced chayote
⅓   cup frozen petite peas, thawed
Kosher salt and freshly ground black pepper to taste
1   cup vegetable broth
¾   cup couscous

1. Heat the oil in a medium skillet to medium-high. Add the onion, garlic, carrot, bell pepper and chayote; sauté until softened, about 5 minutes. Remove from heat and stir in the peas. Season with salt and pepper and set aside.

2. Bring the broth to a boil in a small saucepan and then remove from heat. Pour the couscous into a medium bowl and stir in the vegetables. Pour the hot broth over the couscous. Cover the bowl with a lid or plastic wrap. Let stand for 10 to 15 minutes. Fluff the mixture with a fork. Taste, adjust the seasonings, and serve.

Chayote, a native Mexican plant, is a member of the squash family. The most common type of this starchy squash is pale green with a smooth skin. It has become quite popular in the United States and can be found in most grocery stores. It will keep in a refrigerator for a month or so. If you cannot find it in your market, any summer squash may be substituted.

Chipotle Double-Cooked Potatoes

SERVES 6

3   **medium baking potatoes, scrubbed**

½   **pound soft goat cheese**

½   **cup thinly sliced scallions**

2   **tablespoons puréed chipotles en adobo**

3   **tablespoons unsalted butter**

½   **cup milk**

Salt and freshly ground white pepper

1. Preheat the oven to 350° F.

2. Bake the potatoes for 1 hour, or until done. Let them cool at room temperature. When cool enough to handle, cut potatoes in half lengthwise and hollow out the potatoes, leaving the shells whole and reserving. Mash the potato flesh with the goat cheese, scallions and chipotle puree.

3. In a small saucepan over medium heat, melt the butter with the milk. Beat into the potato-cheese mixture. Season to taste with salt and pepper. Stuff the reserved shells with the potato mixture. Recipe may be prepared up to this point earlier in the day, and then reserved, covered, at room temperature or refrigerated. If refrigerated, bring to room temperature before reheating.

4. To serve, preheat the oven to 400° F. Place the stuffed potatoes on a baking sheet and bake for 5 minutes, or until hot.

CHEESE GRITS

SERVES 8

3   cups water
1   cup milk
1   tablespoon salt
1   cup grits
2   eggs, beaten
Approximately 2 cups
**   shredded cheese (1 cup**
**   goat cheese may be**
**   substituted)**
1   cup New Mexican green
**   chile (optional)**

This recipe was contributed by our own native Texan, Allen Smith, who was a chef on our staff for many years. Most of us here at the school like the addition of 1 cup roasted, chopped New Mexican green chile, but we aren't sure if Allen would approve! We will let you make that decision on your own.

1. In a medium saucepan, bring the water and milk to a boil with the salt.

2. Slowly stir the grits into the boiling liquid. Let cook for 30 to 40 minutes (unless using quick grits, then follow the package directions).

3. Combine the eggs, cheese and chile, if using. Stir into the grits.

4. Pour into a buttered 2-quart baking dish and bake at 350° F for about 30 minutes.

Hominy corn, or posole, has been boiled in a lime solution, then washed and drained before further processing. In Mexico and the Southwest, the treated corn is ground to produce masa, which is what we use to make corn tortillas. In Texas and the Southern United States, it is ground to produce grits.

Marinated Purple Potatoes

SERVES 8

2   pounds purple potatoes, skin on, quartered

½   cup extra virgin olive oil

½   cup finely diced red onion

4   cloves garlic, minced

3   tablespoons sherry vinegar

Kosher salt and freshly ground black pepper to taste

2   tablespoons chopped parsley

Chile caribe to taste (optional)

¼   cup crumbled queso fresco or ricotta

The intense, eye-catching color of this salad really sets it apart from the traditional potato salad that is more typically served. It used to be more difficult to find purple potatoes, but they seem to be appearing more frequently at local grocery stores. Purple potatoes are medium sized, oval and have an assertive, earthy flavor.

1. Boil potatoes until tender, but firm, about 20 minutes. Drain.

2. Warm the oil over medium heat and sauté onion and garlic until softened, about 5 minutes. Add the vinegar and pour mixture over the warm potatoes. Toss with salt, pepper and parsley. Add chile caribe, if using, and mix well. Let stand at room temperature for 1 hour. Sprinkle with cheese before serving.

James Campbell Caruso contributed this recipe from *El Farol: Tapas and Spanish Cuisine* (Gibbs Smith, Publisher, 2004).

Green Rice

SERVES 6 (MAKES ABOUT 3 CUPS)

3 poblano chiles, roasted, peeled and seeded with stems removed

2¼ cups chicken broth, divided

½ cup coarsely chopped cilantro, packed

½ cup coarsely chopped fresh Italian parsley, packed

1 teaspoon dried epazote

3 tablespoons olive oil

1 cup long grain rice

1 cup finely chopped onion

1½ tablespoons minced garlic

1 cup water

1 teaspoon kosher salt

Arroz Verde, or Green Rice, was introduced into Mexico quite early in the colonial period, brought over from the Philippines. It is now an integral part of the everyday Mexican diet. We recommend using a long grain rice for this recipe. Do not use converted or precooked rice as it will not produce the right texture.

1. Combine the chiles and 3/4 cup of the chicken broth in a small saucepan and bring to a boil. Cover the pan, reduce heat to low, and simmer chiles for 12 to 15 minutes, until very soft. Pour the chiles and any broth from the pan into a blender. Add the cilantro, parsley, epazote and 1/2 cup more chicken broth and process until smooth.

2. Heat the oil in a 2-quart saucepan over medium heat. Add rice and onion and cook, stirring frequently, until the rice is no longer translucent and has turned opaque white, about 5 minutes. Stir in the garlic and sauté 1 minute longer.

3. Add the chile puree, remaining broth, water and salt. Stir the mixture, bring to a boil and cover the rice. Reduce heat to a bare simmer and cook for 30 minutes. Turn off the heat, stir the rice, cover and let stand for 5 to 10 minutes. Serve.

What size of rice to use?! Long grain rice when cooked produces light, dry grains that separate easily. They have a dryish, almost mealy texture. Short grain rice has fat, almost round grains that have a higher starch content. When cooked, it tends to be moist and viscous, causing the grains to stick together. Medium grain rice, as expected, has a size and character between the other two. Though fairly fluffy right after it is cooked, medium grain rice tends to clump once it begins to cool.

Spicy Pinto Beans

SERVES 6 TO 8

1   **pound dry pinto beans, picked over for dirt or stones**

8   **thick slices bacon, cut crosswise into ½-inch strips**

1   **medium white onion, diced**

Fresh jalapeño or serrano chiles, dried chipotle chiles or chipotles en adobo to taste

Salt to taste

Splash of balsamic vinegar

Pinch of epazote

2   **tablespoons gold tequila**

⅓   **cup chopped cilantro**

1. Rinse the beans and put them in a 6-quart pot with 6 cups water. Remove any beans that float. Add half the bacon and bring to a boil. Reduce the heat to medium-low and gently simmer, partially covered, until the beans are tender, about 2 to 2 1/2 hours. Stir the beans regularly and add water as necessary to keep the liquid at least 1/2 inch above the level of the beans.

2. Fry the remaining bacon, stirring regularly. Add the onion and chiles, and fry until golden brown, about 10 minutes. Scrape the onion mixture into the beans, then taste and season with salt, vinegar and epazote. Continue simmering, stirring occasionally, for about 30 minutes to blend the flavors. If the beans seem too soupy, boil over medium-high heat, stirring, until desired consistency is reached.

3. Just before serving, stir in the tequila and cilantro.

Corn Flan

SERVES 8 TO 10

6	tablespoons unsalted butter
½	cup bread crumbs
6	cups fresh or thawed frozen corn kernels, divided
2	cups heavy cream, divided
2	teaspoons corn starch
1	cup green chile or 2 tablespoons chipotles en adobo
½	cup thinly sliced green onions
1	clove garlic, peeled and minced
1	tablespoon chopped fresh marjoram or sage
4	large eggs, well beaten
1	cup grated Monterey Jack, cheddar or fontina cheese (may be combined with cojita, romano or Asiago for a sharper flavor)
1	teaspoon salt and black pepper or to taste

This dish is similar to spoonbread or pudding. It is very soft and custard like. It makes a nice side dish, but it would also work well as a breakfast dish garnished with sliced avocado and salsa fresca. This can be made ahead of time, refrigerated and cooked right before you are ready to serve.

1. Preheat oven to 350° F. Lightly butter a 9 x 13-inch baking dish or 10 individual ramekins.

2. Melt the butter and combine a third of it with the bread crumbs. Set aside.

3. In a food processor, puree half the corn with half the cream, corn starch and chile.

4. In the pan with the remaining butter, add green onions and sauté for 2 minutes. Add garlic and marjoram or sage and cook for 2 minutes more.

5. Place all corn, corn puree, onion and garlic in a bowl and mix well. Stir in eggs, cheese and remaining cream. Season with salt and pepper. Pour mixture into a prepared baking dish or ramekins.

6. Sprinkle with bread crumbs. Bake 45 to 50 minutes for a baking dish, 35 to 40 minutes for ramekins.

Twice-Fried Plantains

SERVES 4

2   cups canola oil or
      enough to fry
4   ripe plantains
Salt to taste

Carmen Rodriguez developed this tasty dish to accompany his Brazilian Carnaval menu, which makes sense, as plantains are very popular in Latin countries. Plantains are large and firm and often referred to as the cooking banana. Whereas a banana is eaten ripe, a plantain is typically used while green. It has a mild almost squash-like flavor and is used very much as a potato would be, as a vegetable side dish.

1. Heat oil over medium-high heat to 375° F.
2. Peel plantains and slice into 1-inch pieces. Fry in oil until golden. Remove plantains from the oil and smash with the back side of a small plate or coffee mug. Return to hot oil and cook until crispy.
3. Sprinkle with salt when removed from oil and serve with Mango Salsa.

Mango Salsa

3   ripe mangos
1   red bell pepper, diced
1   small red onion,
      chopped
1   to 2 jalapeños, seeded
      and diced
¼   cup coarsely chopped
      cilantro
2   tablespoons lime juice
      or to taste
2   tablespoons sugar (if
      needed)
Salt to taste

1. Peel the mangos and cut the flesh away from the large, flat pit. Dice the mango into 1/4-inch dice and place in a non-reactive bowl.
2. Add all other ingredients and toss together.
3. Let the salsa stand at room temperature for 15 to 20 minutes to let the flavors meld.

Rice Tumbado

SERVES 6

2   tablespoons olive oil
2   cups white rice
½   cup chopped onion
½   cup chopped celery
½   cup chopped carrot
1   teaspoon minced garlic
2   tablespoons azafran or ⅛ teaspoon Spanish saffron
1   tablespoon kosher salt
3½ cups water or chicken stock
¼   cup coarsely chopped cilantro

Noe Cano contributed this recipe that his mom used to make for him when growing up in Chachltianguls, Vera Cruz, Mexico, which is on the coast and famous for great seafood. Traditionally it is a seafood rice dish that is just "thrown together," as its name tells us it should be. However, since we serve this dish with a fish main course, we have eliminated the seafood. You could also toss in peas in addition to the onion, celery and carrots.

1. Warm the oil in a 2-quart saucepan over medium-high heat. Add the rice and stir until the grains are opaque and beginning to color, 3 to 4 minutes. Stir in the onion, celery and carrot; continue to cook for 3 to 4 minutes. Add the garlic, azafran and salt along with the water or stock; stir to combine.

2. Bring the mixture to a boil, reduce heat to low and cover. Cook for 20 minutes. Remove from heat and allow to stand 10 minutes before removing the cover. Stir in cilantro and serve.

HERBED CHICKEN BREASTS

ANCHO CHILE RELLENO WITH SPICY TOMATO SAUCE

FIERY TURKEY FILLETS

FLAUTAS WITH SALSA VERDE AND SALSA ROJA

CHIPOTLE-MARINATED STEAK FAJITAS

VERACRUZ-STYLE FISH

CHILE RELLENO WITH GOAT CHEESE

Main Dishes

Lamb Adovada with Chipotle Chile Sauce & Carmelized Corn

SERVES 10

2   teaspoons coriander seeds

2   teaspoons cumin seeds

1   teaspoon whole black peppercorns

8   medium cloves garlic

3   to 4 teaspoons salt

4   tablespoons Chimayo or ancho chile powder

2   teaspoons Mexican oregano

2   teaspoons dried thyme

1   teaspoon ground canela

½   cup cider vinegar

2   tablespoons olive oil

3   racks of lamb (2 to 2½ pounds each, 7 or 8 chops per rack), or leg of lamb (6 to 8 pounds), well trimmed of fat

Many people have never shown much enthusiasm for lamb. On average, Americans consume a pound of lamb per person annually, a fraction of our beef consumption. However, once you try this you will be converted! Guests at the school are surprised how much they like this lamb and confess to enjoying more lamb since their discovery. It works well for a dinner party because it is elegant, but you can get the rub on the lamb in the morning and there isn't a lot of last-minute preparation. You can make the chipotle sauce ahead of time and freeze it if you like—careful—this sauce has a kick to it!

1. Toast the coriander seeds, cumin seeds and peppercorns in a small, heavy skillet over moderate heat, stirring until the spices are fragrant and begin to brown, about 2 minutes. Transfer spices to a plate to cool. Using a mortar and pestle, crush the toasted spices with the garlic and salt to make a coarse paste. Mix in the chile powder, oregano, thyme and canela. Stir in the vinegar and oil until well blended. Rub the spice mixture over the lamb and allow to stand at room temperature for at least 1 hour, or cover and refrigerate overnight. (Remove meat from refrigerator at least 1 hour before cooking.)

2. Preheat the oven to 450° F.

3. In a large roasting pan, roast the lamb for 10 minutes. Lower the temperature to 375° F and cook until a meat thermometer inserted in the thickest part of the lamb (without touching the bone) reads 140° F (for medium-rare). Transfer the lamb to a carving board, cover loosely with foil and let rest for 15 minutes before slicing. Serve with Chipotle Chile Sauce and garnish with Caramelized Corn.

(continued on page 114)

Spanish explorer Francisco Coronado brought sheep into the Southwest in 1540. Lamb is the traditional meat of the area. Rumor has it there was a time when more lamb was shipped out of northern New Mexico yearly than anywhere else in the world. These days there are very few people raising sheep in the area. One family, Molly Manzanares and her husband, Antonio, has maintained their family tradition of sheep raising. They created a company called Shepherds Lamb, where they work to preserve traditions and stimulate economic development in northern New Mexico. They provide certified organic lamb to many of Santa Fe's restaurants and sell it at the Farmers Market.

Chipotle Chile Sauce

2 tablespoons olive oil
4 medium cloves garlic, minced
2 cups canned tomatoes, drained
1 teaspoon salt
3 to 4 tablespoons pureed chipotles en adobo
Salt to taste

1. Heat the oil in a medium skillet. Add the garlic and sauté for 1 minute. Add the tomatoes, breaking them up with a spoon. Stir in the salt and cook over high heat, stirring occasionally, until the liquid has reduced to 1 1/2 cups or less, about 5 minutes.

2. Transfer the mixture to a blender or food processor. Add the chipotles and puree. Season with salt.

Caramelized Corn

2 cups baby corn kernels, cut from the cob or frozen
3 tablespoons balsamic vinegar
Salt and pepper to taste

1. Heat a large, heavy skillet over medium-high heat. Add the corn and stir until the kernels begin to brown. Add balsamic vinegar, salt and pepper and continue to cook for 1 minute.

Tandoori Fish with Coconut Chutney

SERVES 6

6 skinless fish fillets, preferably red snapper or rock fish

Salt and pepper to taste

1 cup plain yogurt

1 tablespoon minced ginger

1 tablespoon minced garlic

1 tablespoon Chimayo chile powder

1½ teaspoons achiote paste

1 teaspoon ground cumin

1 teaspoon ground coriander

Juice of 1 lime

6 banana leaves cut in 6-inch squares and 6 strips for tying

World traveler Rocky Durham developed this recipe as part of a Carnaval celebration. It comes from Trinidad in the Caribbean but uses many of the spices familiar to this region.

1. Season both sides of fish with salt and pepper.

2. Combine remaining ingredients (except banana leaves) in a bowl and mix well to combine.

3. Cover fish in yogurt mixture and let stand for at least 1 hour.

4. Wrap individual fish fillets in banana leaves and fold in the sides and then the top and bottom. Tie with strips and and bake for approximately 20 minutes at 375° F or until cooked through. It can be cooked on the grill as well.

5. Serve with Coconut Chutney.

Coconut Chutney

2 cups shredded, sweetened coconut

1½ cups pineapple, diced

5 chiles de arbol, stems and seeds removed

½ cup coconut milk

1 tablespoon brown sugar

1 tablespoon curry powder

1 teaspoon toasted ground coriander (see p. 144 for toasting spices)

1 lime, juiced and zested

1 tablespoon chopped fresh mint

1 tablespoon chopped fresh basil

1 tablespoon chopped fresh cilantro

1. Toast the shredded coconut in a preheated 350° F oven until golden brown (approximately 2 minutes).

2. Combine the coconut, pineapple, chiles, coconut milk, brown sugar, curry powder, coriander and lime juice in a saucepan and simmer for 30 minutes.

3. Add zest and herbs and simmer for 3 or 4 minutes more. Remove from heat and let cool.

SWEET & SPICY BABY BACK RIBS

SERVES 4 TO 6

MARINADE

8	garlic cloves, unpeeled
6	dried ancho chiles, stemmed and seeded
8	dried New Mexican or guajillo chiles stemmed and seeded
¾	cup broth or water, plus more if needed
2	tablespoons chipotles en adobo
2	teaspoons dried Mexican oregano
½	teaspoon toasted ground cumin
½	teaspoon freshly ground black pepper
1	teaspoon Santa Fe Seasons Sweet Spices or 1 teaspoon ground canela and a pinch of cloves and allspice
⅛	cup apple cider vinegar

Salt to taste

1	to 2 tablespoons brown sugar

RIBS

4	to 6 pounds pork baby back ribs
2	tablespoons brown sugar or to taste

Water or broth as needed

FOR THE MARINADE

1. Heat a heavy skillet over medium and roast the garlic turning occasionally until blackened and soft, about 10 minutes. Cool and peel.

2. Raise the heat slightly on the skillet and toast the chiles on the hot surface, pressing with a metal spatula until they start to crackle, then turn them and toast the other side. Be careful not to burn the chiles. Place the chiles in a small bowl and cover them with boiling water. Let soak for 20 to 30 minutes, drain and discard the water.

3. Blend the chiles along with the broth, chipotle, oregano, cumin, black pepper and Sweet Spice. Add vinegar. Add more liquid as needed to make a smooth puree. Strain into a bowl and add salt and brown sugar to taste.

FOR THE RIBS

1. Place the ribs in a long roasting pan and paint them with half of the marinade. Cover and refrigerate for several hours or overnight. Add the brown sugar to the remaining marinade, cover with tin foil and refrigerate for several hours.

2. Preheat the oven to 350° F. Uncover ribs and add water or broth to a depth of about 1/4 inch and replace the foil. Bake for approximately 45 minutes. Uncover and return the ribs to the oven for an additional 30 minutes. Skim the fat and pour off any excess liquid.

3. To glaze, raise the oven temperature to 450° or heat a grill. Brush the ribs heavily with the remaining marinade and bake until they are a deep red color, about 20 minutes. Boil any excess marinade and serve with the ribs.

Roast Pork Loin with Red Chile–Peanut Mole

SERVES 8 TO 10

2	teaspoons black peppercorns
2	teaspoons kosher salt
3	bay leaves
2	teaspoons dried Mexican oregano
2	teaspoons freshly toasted cumin seeds
2	teaspoons freshly toasted coriander seeds
4-	to 5-pound boneless, center-cut pork loin
3	tablespoons olive oil

1. Grind all spices in a spice grinder or with a mortar and pestle. Rub the spice mixture over the surface of the pork loin. Wrap the loin in plastic and refrigerate for 24 to 48 hours.

2. Preheat the oven to 375° F.

3. Heat the oil in a large skillet over medium-high heat. Sear the pork on all sides until browned. Transfer to a foil-lined baking sheet and roast in the oven until the internal temperature reads 160° F, about 1 1/2 hours. Allow the pork to rest for 15 to 20 minutes before slicing. Serve with Red Chile-Peanut Mole.

What is mole? This should be in the most frequently asked questions section of the book, but we didn't add it there as it is not a brief answer. Typically, people think of a sauce made of chocolate and chile. This is not entirely wrong but probably not the best explanation either. Mole literally means "sauce." Moles are often thickened with ground nuts or seeds. Moles usually have chiles in them. Moles often have chocolate in them, but not always. Moles are generally made for special occasions. Does this confuse you more? You can't oversimplify what mole is. There is red mole, black mole, green mole and yellow mole. Even though there are so many different recipes for mole, all of them will have some or all of the components of the above-mentioned items.

Red Chile–Peanut Mole

12 dried ancho chiles
2   tablespoons olive oil
1   large onion, chopped
6   unpeeled cloves garlic, roasted, then peeled
4   large, ripe tomatoes, roasted
¾   cup dry roasted peanuts
⅓   cup toasted sliced almonds
⅓   cup toasted sesame seeds, ground to a powder in a spice grinder
1   or 2 teaspoons espresso powder, or to taste
1   to 2 teaspoons each freshly ground cumin, coriander, canela and allspice, or to taste
4   tablespoons lard or olive oil
Salt to taste
Chipotle chile powder to taste

1. In a preheated skillet over medium heat, press the chiles, 3 or 4 at a time, onto the bottom of the pan until fragrant and pliable. Be careful not to burn them. Remove the stems and tear the softened flesh into large pieces, removing the seeds that stick to the flesh. Soak the chile pieces in hot water for 30 minutes, until softened.

2. In the meantime, heat the oil in a small skillet and sauté the onion until softened. Place the sautéed onion, garlic cloves and tomatoes in a blender and puree. Pour mixture into a bowl and set aside. Return 1 cup of this mixture to the blender and add the peanuts, almonds and sesame seed powder. Puree, adding a little of the tomato liquid, if necessary. Combine the pureed tomato mixture and the peanut mixture, and add the espresso powder and spices.

3. Drain the chiles, reserving the soaking liquid. Place the chile pieces in a blender and add 1/2 cup of the soaking liquid, or more if needed. Puree until thoroughly blended. Add the chile puree to the other purees and stir to combine thoroughly.

4. In a large saucepan, heat the lard. When it is hot, add the puree all at once. You may want to use the lid of the pan as a shield, as the liquid will splatter. Bring the mixture to a boil, reduce the heat, season with salt and chipotle chile powder, and simmer for 30 minutes, stirring occasionally, until you have a sauce the consistency of thick cream.

Spicy Tomato Sauce

2 tablespoons extra virgin olive oil

1 small white onion, finely chopped

2 cloves garlic, minced

1 teaspoon dried Mexican oregano

1 28-ounce can whole tomatoes with juice, pureed

1 15-ounce can diced tomatoes with juice

2 or 3 tablespoons chipotles en adobo, finely chopped, or chipotle seasoning to taste

Pinch of sugar

Kosher salt to taste

1. Warm the oil in a medium saucepan over medium-high heat. Add the onion and sauté until translucent, about 3 minutes. Add the garlic and oregano, and sauté for 1 minute. Add the tomatoes with their juices and the chipotles. Season with sugar and salt to taste. Simmer uncovered until slightly thickened, about 25 to 30 minutes. Set aside until ready to use.

Veracruz-Style Fish

SERVES 6

2½ pounds red snapper fillets, skin removed (halibut or mahimahi may be substituted)

Fresh lime juice

Kosher salt and freshly ground black pepper

Dried Mexican oregano

3 tablespoons extra virgin olive oil

1 large white onion, diced

3 cloves garlic, minced

2 to 3 pickled chiles (jalapeño or serrano), finely chopped

1 28-ounce can whole tomatoes

4 ripe tomatoes

2 tablespoons non-pareil capers, drained

½ cup chopped pimiento-stuffed olives

2 poblano chiles, roasted, peeled, seeded and finely chopped

½ cup sliced almonds, toasted

2 tablespoons snipped fresh chives or scallion tops

¼ cup coarsely chopped cilantro

2 teaspoons ground canela plus 2 whole sticks

1 teaspoon salt

½ teaspoon Mexican oregano

3 cups water, vegetable broth or fish stock

Salt and freshly ground black pepper

2 tablespoons olive oil for searing

Fresh cilantro, for garnish

1. Lay the fish out on a tray and sprinkle with lime juice, salt, pepper and oregano. Cover with plastic wrap and set aside for 30 minutes.

2. Heat the oil in a large pot (4-quart) over medium-high heat. Add the onion and cook until translucent, about 3 minutes. Add the garlic and chiles and sauté 2 minutes. Puree the whole tomatoes in a blender and add to the mixture. Cut the fresh tomatoes in half horizontally and grate the flesh against the large holes of a box grater into a small bowl. Add to the pot along with the remaining ingredients, except the fresh cilantro garnish and oil for searing.

3. Bring the mixture to a simmer and cook, partially covered, for 30 minutes. Taste and adjust seasoning.

4. To serve, preheat the oven to 450° F. Position a rack to just above middle. Add the olive oil to a large nonstick skillet over medium-high heat. Sear the fish fillets on both sides for about 1 1/2 minutes. Transfer the fillets to a foil-covered baking sheet. Place the sheet in the oven on a high rack and roast for 5 minutes. Remove fish from oven and serve each fillet on a portion of rice or Rice Tumbado (see page 109) topped with a ladle of sauce. Garnish with fresh cilantro.

Flautas with Salsa Verde & Salsa Roja

SERVES 10

30 corn tortillas

5 baking potatoes, peeled, cooked in salted water, drained and mashed

1 pound Monterey Jack cheese, grated

1 quart canola oil for frying

Crème fraîche

Crumbled queso fresco or feta cheese

Flautas are little "flutes" of corn tortillas wrapped around the filling of shredded chicken, pork or—in this case, mashed potatoes—and then deep fried. We wanted to keep the filling really simple as to highlight the wonderful sauces that we serve with the flautas. The sauces can be made ahead of time, and they freeze very well.

1. Heat the corn tortillas in a cast-iron skillet to soften. Put 2 tablespoons mashed potato and a sprinkling of cheese in the center of a tortilla. Roll the tortilla into a cigar shape and secure with a toothpick. Repeat with the remaining tortillas. Cover flautas with a towel, or, if not using promptly, place them in a plastic bag and refrigerate for later use.

2. Heat the oil in a frying pan to just under the smoking point (365 to 370° F). Fry the tortillas until crisp and golden, turning to crisp evenly. Drain on paper towels. Keep them warm, if needed, in a 200° F oven for up to 30 minutes.

3. To serve, divide the flautas evenly among ten plates. On each plate, ladle 1/3 cup Salsa Verde over half the flautas and 1/3 cup Salsa Roja over the other half. Drizzle crème fraîche over flautas and sprinkle queso fresco on top.

Salsa Verde (Green Sauce)

MAKES ABOUT 6 CUPS

1½ quarts water

1½ pounds tomatillos, husked, rinsed and cut in half

2 medium white onions, peeled, sliced and divided

9 cloves garlic, peeled and divided

6 serrano chiles, seeds removed, divided

2 bunches cilantro, washed, dried, chopped and divided

4 tablespoons extra virgin olive oil, divided

Salt to taste

1. Bring water to a boil in a saucepan. Add the tomatillos, half the onions, 5 cloves garlic, 3 chiles, and half the chopped cilantro. Simmer for 30 minutes. Cool and drain, reserving the cooking liquid.

2. Heat 2 tablespoons oil in a large skillet over high heat. Fry the remaining onions, garlic, and chiles until browned.

3. In a blender, puree the fried mixture with some of the reserved cooking liquid and transfer to a bowl.

4. Puree the boiled ingredients and add to the fried puree. Heat the remaining oil in a large saucepan over high heat and pour in the pureed mixture. Add enough reserved cooking liquid to achieve a medium consistency, reduce the heat and simmer, stirring frequently, for 30 minutes.

Salsa Roja (Red Sauce)

MAKES ABOUT 6 CUPS

2 pounds ripe Roma tomatoes

2 medium white onions, sliced

6 whole cloves garlic, peeled

1 to 1½ cups tomato juice

½ cup olive oil

Chipotle chile powder to taste

Salt and sugar to taste

1. On a grill, char the Roma tomatoes, half the onion, and half the garlic. Cool. Combine grilled vegetables with remaining onion and garlic. In a blender, in batches, puree the vegetables, adding tomato juice, as needed, to thin.

2. Heat the oil in a large saucepan over high heat. Pour in the pureed vegetables and continue to cook, stirring, until the sauce has slightly thickened. Season to taste with chipotle chile powder, salt and sugar.

NOTE: Freeze any unused sauce and serve later.

Herbed Chicken Breasts with Huitlacoche-Roasted Corn Salsa

SERVES 4

1½ cups buttermilk
Kosher salt and freshly ground black pepper
4   skinless, boneless chicken breast halves
½   cup flour
2   eggs
2   tablespoons water
8   slices firm white bread, crusts removed
2   cloves garlic, minced
Leaves from 2 sprigs fresh rosemary, chopped
1   tablespoon green chile powder
Zest of 1 lemon, minced
4   tablespoons olive oil

We use these simple breaded and fried chicken breasts as a way to showcase this unique, rustic huitlacoche corn salsa. It is difficult to find a word that accurately describes the flavor of huitlacoche. Some have likened it to the flavor of wild morel mushrooms; however, there is simply no way to describe your first bite of this black fungus!

1. Combine buttermilk, salt and pepper in a zipper-lock bag and set aside.

2. Place a chicken breast half between two large squares of parchment or plastic. Using a meat pounder or the bottom of a small skillet, flatten the chicken to a thickness of about 1/3 inch. Repeat with the remaining breasts. Add the chicken breasts to buttermilk mixture in the zipper-lock bag. Chill at least 20 minutes.

3. Preheat oven to 300° F. Put the flour in a shallow dish. Lightly beat the eggs with water in a separate shallow dish. Tear the bread into large pieces and place in the bowl of a food processor. Pulse until fine crumbs form, about 10 seconds. Add the garlic, rosemary, chile powder and lemon zest and pulse to combine thoroughly. Transfer the mixture to a another shallow dish.

4. Remove a chicken breast half from the buttermilk and shake off excess liquid. Dredge both sides of the chicken in the flour, shaking to remove the excess. Coat the floured breasts in the egg wash, then dredge in the seasoned crumbs and transfer to a plate. Repeat with remaining chicken breasts.

5. Line a baking sheet with aluminum foil. Heat a medium nonstick skillet over medium-high heat. Add the olive oil. Sauté 2 chicken breasts until golden on the bottom, about 2 minutes. Turn and cook until golden and cooked through, about 3 to 5 minutes more. Transfer chicken to the baking sheet and keep warm while cooking the remaining chicken. Serve with Huitlacoche-Roasted Corn Salsa.

Huitlacoche-Roasted Corn Salsa

YIELDS 2½ CUPS

3 ears of corn

2 tablespoons canola oil

½ cup diced white onion

2 cloves roasted garlic, very finely chopped

1 cup rich, full-bodied red wine (cabernet, merlot, pinot noir)

½ cup (4 ounces) canned or frozen huitlacoche

1 tablespoon pureed chipotles en adobo

2 teaspoons fresh epazote or 1 teaspoon dried

¼ cup cilantro chiffonade

Kosher salt and freshly ground black pepper to taste

1. Shuck the ears of corn and remove silk. Roast corn over direct flame, turning frequently, until blackened in places and then set aside. When the ears have cooled, cut the kernels from the cob and place them in a bowl. There should be about 1 1/2 cups.

2. Heat the oil in a skillet over medium heat. Add onion and sauté until golden, 4 to 5 minutes. Add garlic and red wine, and reduce by half. Add huitlacoche, chipotle en adobo and epazote and continue to cook over low heat, stirring frequently, for 8 to 10 minutes, until most of the liquid has evaporated. Remove from heat and let cool.

3. Add the roasted corn kernels and cilantro to the "dry" mixture and stir to combine well. Season to taste with salt and pepper.

Huitlacoche is a black fungus that grows in the kernels of corn and causes the kernels to change into unusual shapes and look quite strange. Many places in Mexico consider huitlacoche a delicacy, but it is not so highly regarded in the United States and is often referred to as corn smut.

Smoked Pork Tenderloin with Red Chile–Cider Glaze & Apple–Piñon Chutney

SERVES 8 TO 10

4   cups cool water
⅛   cup kosher or sea salt
⅛   cup sugar
2   tablespoons apple cider vinegar
8   whole peppercorns
4   toasted bay leaves
5   pounds pork tenderloin or 10 pork chops

Daniel Hoyer developed a version of this recipe when designing the menu for the restaurant chain in England called Santa fe. It was one of the most popular items on the menu as it is full of great flavor without being too hot. Daniel, Kathi Long and Rocky Durham developed recipes for the menu at the restaurants and traveled to England to help get things rolling. Needless to say, they had a lot of fun doing it!

1. Combine water, salt, sugar, vinegar, peppercorns and bay leaves in a non-reactive dish. Add pork. Using a plate or heavy object to keep meat immersed, refrigerate for at least 1 hour or up to 24 hours, preferably overnight.

2. Sear meat on a griddle. Place meat in a preheated stovetop smoker and smoke for approximately 20 minutes. Pool the Red Chile–Cider Glaze (see page 130) on individual plates and top with sliced pork or pork chop. Garnish with Apple–Piñon Chutney (see page 130).

Optional cooking method: Cook meat on grill or in an oven at 400° F until desired doneness, brushing several times with glaze.

(continued on page 130)

STOVETOP SMOKER
This recipe is greatly enhanced by the use of a stovetop smoker—a metal container with a sliding metal lid that is designed to sit on top of the burners on everyday cooktops. The heat source ignites the wood chips or wood dust, generating smoke. The added flavor is incredible for such a simple device.

Red Chile–Cider Glaze

YIELDS 2 CUPS

½ gallon apple cider or juice
3 tablespoons honey
⅛ cup sugar
4 cloves garlic
6 allspice berries or 1 tablespoon ground allspice
1 teaspoon toasted coriander seeds
2 bay leaves, toasted
4 whole cloves
1 stick canela
½ teaspoon salt
3 tablespoons Chimayo red chile powder
3 tablespoons toasted ancho chile powder
1 tablespoon vegetable oil
2 tablespoons cider vinegar

Combine ingredients in heavy saucepan and boil until reduced by half. Lower the heat and reduce to half again. This should take between 45 minutes and 1 hour. The mixture should be the consistency of maple syrup. Strain to remove solids.

Apple–Piñon Chutney

YIELDS 2 CUPS

2 cups fresh, peeled green apples, cut into ½-inch dice (½ cup reserved)
½ cup diced onions
1 clove garlic, sliced
1 cup apple cider
⅓ cup cider vinegar
¾ cup water
¼ cup red chile honey
2 tablespoons Red Chile–Cider Glaze
Pinch of salt
½ teaspoon ground allspice
1 teaspoon ground canela
¼ cup raisins or dried currants
½ cup toasted piñon nuts
Juice of ½ lime or lemon

1. Place all ingredients except reserved apples, raisins, piñon nuts and lime juice in a heavy saucepan and bring to a boil. Allow liquid to reduce by about half. This should take about 30 minutes. Add reserved apples and raisins.

2. Reduce heat to simmer and continue cooking until liquid has evaporated.

3. Stir in the piñon nuts, cool 5 minutes, add lime juice and adjust the seasonings. Serve warm or at room temperature.

CHILE RELLENO WITH GOAT CHEESE & MUSHROOMS

SERVES 8

½ pound diced shiitake, white or other wild mushrooms

2 tablespoons olive oil

12 ounces mild goat cheese

6 ounces cream cheese, at room temperature

2 tablespoons chopped fresh marjoram

1 bunch green onions, chopped

8 roasted and peeled New Mexico green chiles, with seeds removed; keep intact and cut a slit down three-fourths the length of the side

1 cup blue cornmeal

½ cup all-purpose flour

1 teaspoon salt

1 tablespoon New Mexico (Chimayo) red chile powder

2 egg yolks

2 tablespoons cold water

1. Sauté mushrooms in very hot oil until caramelized. Cool and mix with the cheeses, marjoram and onions.

2. Stuff chiles with mixture, squeezing to shape.

3. Refrigerate for at least 15 minutes.

4. Mix together cornmeal, flour, salt and chile.

5. Whip egg yolks with 2 tablespoons water.

6. Dip chiles in egg wash and coat with blue cornmeal mix.

7. Cook on a lightly oiled griddle or in a heavy skillet until golden brown.

FIERY TURKEY FILLETS WITH ROASTED PINEAPPLE SALSA

SERVES 6 TO 8

3   pounds turkey fillets, well trimmed

1   tablespoon ancho chile powder

2   tablespoons pureed chipotles en adobo

3   tablespoons Chimayo chile powder

¼   cup finely minced onions

1   tablespoon minced garlic

½   cup coarsely chopped cilantro

1   tablespoon dried Mexican oregano

½   teaspoon toasted and ground cumin

⅔   cup freshly squeezed lime juice

2   tablespoons extra virgin olive oil

⅓   cup white wine

1   teaspoon salt

Although no longer living in Santa Fe, Janet Mitchell, while teaching at the School, developed this recipe for one of our light menu classes. It has become one of our family favorites, particularly in the summer as it works well on the grill. You don't have to sacrifice flavor for healthy food in this recipe.

1. Rinse fillets quickly under running water and pat dry with paper towels. Place in a large plastic food storage bag.

2. Combine all remaining ingredients in a small bowl to make a marinade. Stir well. Pour over turkey and turn to coat thoroughly. Refrigerate for up to 2 hours.

3. Allow turkey to return to room temperature before cooking. Remove from marinade, scraping off any excess. Pour marinade into small saucepan and simmer over low heat for 3 minutes.

4. Grill or broil fillets 5 to 6 minutes per side, or until the desired doneness is achieved, brushing occasionally with marinade. Slice the fillets into medallions. Spoon a few tablespoons of heated marinade on individual serving plates, and fan out the turkey medallions over top. Serve with Roasted Pineapple Salsa.

ROASTED PINEAPPLE SALSA

1   fresh pineapple
1   red bell pepper, diced
½   cup chopped cilantro
½   cup minced red onion
2   tablespoons minced jalapeño chiles
1   tablespoon seasoned rice vinegar or white wine vinegar
1   teaspoon olive oil
1   teaspoon Howlin' Hot Sauce or your favorite hot sauce
1   teaspoon salt

1. Peel, core and slice the pineapple into 1/4-inch slices and grill until lightly browned on both sides. Dice pineapple (should yield approximately 2 cups depending on the size).

2. Mix all the ingredients together and stir well to combine. Serve as soon as possible as the brightness of the colors tends to fade with time.

New Mexico Wines

Nearly 400 years ago, Franciscan priests secured safe passage for a revered plant along the dusty trails of the Camino Real (King's Highway) from Mexico into what would later become New Mexico. These bundles of sticks, wrapped with moist soil in swatches of cloth, were neither crops to feed settlers nor medicinal balms to sooth the wounds of conquistadors, but rather grapevine cuttings that would become instrumental in establishing the first vineyards in the future United States.

These grapes of the species Vitis vinifera are believed to be of the variety known as "Monica" in Spain. This "Mission grape" as it came to be known in the New World, was cultivated primarily for sacramental wine at missions along the Rio Grande valley. While it lacked the acidity and color for good table wine, the grape was certainly acceptable for its intended purpose. Furthermore, this hardy and drought-resistant grape was perfect for experimentation in the New Mexico climate—known for extremes in weather, altitude and terrain.

Despite the harshness of New Mexico's environs, wine production is possible because many pests cannot survive in the arid climate, nor can rot, mold or mildew; cold temperatures at high altitudes also interrupt the life cycle of insects, resulting in favorable condi-tions for Vitis vinifera. In addition, New Mexico boasts plentiful sunny days and cool nights. Nighttime temperature drops of 30 to 35 degrees Fahrenheit enable grapes to main-tain the high acid–to–high sugar balance essential for good wine.

For several hundred years, vintners experi-mented with old- and new-world grapes—blending the vinifera grape that is the basis of all great wines with hardier but less flavorful Vitis labrusca (a native American grape) to produce what are known as French-hybrids. These are popular with New Mexico wine-makers and contribute to several delicious blends. Examples include the French-hybrid red Leon Millot, used in La Chiripada's Vintner's Reserve Red, as well as the French-hybrid white Vidal Blanc, used in Ponderosa Valley Vineyard's Summer Sage.

Near the end of the nineteenth century, New Mexico produced 908,000 gallons of wine, ranking as one of the top producers in North America. However, a variety of events—including prohibition and the Depression—caused the commercial industry to topple and remain inactive for nearly fifty years. A renais-sance began in the 1970s and continues to this day. At present, New Mexico produces well over one million gallons of wine annually and is home to nearly two dozen wineries.

Recently, New Mexico wines have piqued the interest of enthusiasts nationwide. In 2002, Gruet's Brut N/V earned a rating of 89 from Wine Enthusiast—placing it in the top fifty. Wine Spectator awarded Casa Rondeña's 2002 Cabernet Franc its highest rating of any New Mexico wine, and La Chiripada garnered a bronze medal at the 2004 International Eastern Wine Competition with their Vintner's Reserve Red 2002.

Nonetheless, ask any wine-loving acquaintance from the West Coast about New Mexico wines and they will likely inform you that such incarnations do not exist or, if they did, you would surely not want to drink them. But never mind skeptics. Wine is a drink best enjoyed in a relaxed state and with an open, adventurous mind. Whether as a complement to food or accompaniment to good company, wine simply adds a little extra something that can turn routine life into satisfying lifestyle. You'll never know until you try. So enjoy a crisp Sauvignon Blanc on a sunny patio, pair a supple Pinot Noir with stuffed quail or share a hearty blend of French-hybrids with friends and red chile enchiladas—you just might find yourself enchanted.

—*By Severn Thomas*

Goat Cheese Enchiladas with Tomatillo Sauce

SERVES 8

- 1½ pounds fresh goat cheese
- ¼ pound shredded asadero cheese (or Monterey Jack)
- 1 tablespoon dried epazote
- 1 teaspoon freshly ground black pepper

SAUCE

- 1 yellow onion, diced
- 1 tablespoon olive oil
- 4 cloves garlic, minced
- ½ gallon tomatillos (about 35), husks removed and quartered
- 4 poblano chiles, roasted, peeled, seeded and then cut into strips
- 6 cups chicken or vegetable stock
- 1 bunch fresh cilantro

Salt and pepper

ASSEMBLY

- 16 corn tortillas (heated in oil until soft and pliable)
- ¼ pound asadero cheese (see sidebar p. 138)

This is one of the few times we will say this: use store-bought corn tortillas. If you use homemade corn tortillas, they tear when rolled. If you want to use corn tortillas made from scratch, you will have to stack your enchiladas instead of roll them.

FOR ENCHILADAS

In a mixing bowl, blend the cheeses, epazote and pepper. Set aside.

FOR TOMATILLO SAUCE

In a large saucepan, sauté onion in oil until translucent. Add garlic, tomatillos and poblanos. Stir and sauté for 2 minutes. Add stock and bring to a boil for 5 minutes. Reduce heat to simmer for about 15 minutes. Chop the cilantro and add it to the sauce just before pureeing in a blender or food processor. Add salt and pepper to taste.

FOR ASSEMBLY

Pour 1 cup Tomatillo Sauce in a glass or ceramic casserole and spread evenly on bottom. Fill tortillas with 3 to 4 tablespoons of cheese mixture. Roll the filled tortillas and place in the casserole seam side down. Cover with remaining Tomatillo Sauce. Sprinkle with asadero cheese. Bake at 350° F for 10 to 15 minutes.

Shredded Pork Tacos

YIELDS FILLING FOR 24 TACOS

2   pounds boneless pork shoulder, cut into 2-inch cubes
3   cloves garlic, peeled and diced
1   large white onion, finely chopped, divided
3   sprigs fresh marjoram
3   cloves garlic, unpeeled
1¼ pounds ripe Roma tomatoes
1   to 2 teaspoons pureed chipotles en adobo
4   tablespoons olive or vegetable oil, divided
1   teaspoon Mexican oregano
1   teaspoon freshly ground canela
½   teaspoon freshly ground black pepper
¼   teaspoon ground cloves
¾   cup Zante currants or golden raisins
¾   cup toasted, sliced almonds
Sea salt to taste
Fresh corn tortillas
Salsa and/or hot sauce

1. Place the pork in a large saucepan and cover with water by several inches. Salt the water liberally. Add 3 cloves diced garlic, half the onion and marjoram to the pan. Bring the water to a boil, skim the foam, reduce the heat and simmer for 1 1/2 to 2 hours, partially covered, until the pork is very tender. Cool the meat in its broth. Shred the pork and reserve.

2. Toast 3 cloves unpeeled garlic in a small skillet over medium-high heat, turning occasionally, until soft, 8 to 10 minutes. Cool and peel. Roast the tomatoes on an Santa Fe School of Cooking grill until charred on all sides. Cool and peel, saving any juices.

3. Place the tomatoes and juices, chipotles en adobo and garlic in the blender and puree. Heat 2 tablespoons oil in a medium saucepan over medium-high heat. Pour in the puree and stir as it thickens, about 7 minutes. Season with salt.

4. Heat the remaining oil in a large nonstick pan over medium-high heat. Add the shredded pork and the remaining onion. Fry the mixture, stirring frequently, until it is browned and slightly crispy, about 15 minutes. Add the oregano, canela, pepper and cloves and stir for 1 minute. Pour on the sauce, add the currants, and stir occasionally until almost all the liquid has evaporated, about 6 to 8 minutes. Stir in the almonds. Taste and adjust seasonings.

5. To serve, scoop about 1/4 cup filling into warmed corn tortillas or place the filling in a bowl and serve a basket of warmed tortillas for the guests to make their own tacos. Serve salsa or hot sauce separately.

CHORIZO ENCHILADAS WITH GUAJILLO SAUCE

SERVES 8

If you can purchase good quality chorizo, use the following:

1¾ **pounds chorizo**

½ **yellow onion, diced**

1½ **tablespoons chipotles en adobo**

¼ **cup roasted peanut oil**

1½ **cups cooked potatoes, diced**

FOR ASSEMBLY

6 **cups Guajillo Chile Sauce, divided**

16 **corn tortillas (heated in oil until soft and pliable)**

1 **cup shredded asadero or Monterey Jack cheese**

These enchiladas are from one of our Cuisines of Mexico classes and really highlight some of the main differences between Mexican and New Mexican styles of food. The sauce here is made with guajillo chiles, one of the most common chiles grown in Mexico. Any red chile sauce in New Mexico would be made with Chimayo chile or other New Mexico red chiles, such as Sandia. Also, you will notice that the enchiladas are rolled. Here in New Mexico, it is more traditional to serve our enchiladas flat or stacked.

1. If using purchased chorizo, combine with onion and chipotles en adobo.

2. Heat a heavy skillet and add the oil. Cook the chorizo mixture over medium heat for 10 minutes, or until cooked through. Stir in the cooked potatoes and remove from heat. Taste and adjust seasoning, if needed.

3. To assemble, pour 1 cup Guajillo Chile Sauce in a large glass or ceramic casserole. Fill 16 corn tortillas each with 3 to 4 tablespoons of the chorizo and potato mixture. Roll and place seam side down in the casserole. Cover with remaining Guajillo Chile Sauce and sprinkle cheese over top. Bake at 350° F for 10 to 15 minutes.

MEXICAN CHEESES

People often think of Mexican food as food covered in melted cheese. Most dishes in authentic Mexican cooking are in fact cheeseless or simply sprinkled with a cheese, not melted over it. The two Mexican cheeses that we use at the school are usually queso fresco and asadero. Queso fresco is similar to fresh goat cheese in that it won't melt and has a very fresh taste. However, it is usually drier and saltier. Asadero is a rich melting cheese that is very mild with a soft but slightly chewy consistency. It is often used on quesadillas and in chile rellenos. It is very difficult to find good-quality Mexican cheeses in the U.S. That being said, if you need to substitute, the closest cheese you will find to queso fresco would be feta. If you can't find asadero, go ahead and use Monterey Jack.

Guajillo Chile Sauce

YIELDS ABOUT 8 CUPS

10 to 12 guajillo chiles
½ cup olive oil
½ yellow onion, diced
4 cloves garlic, minced
4 tablespoons flour
1 tablespoon toasted and ground coriander
1 teaspoon toasted and ground cumin
6 cups chicken stock
4 Roma tomatoes, halved lengthwise and roasted on grill or in oven until lightly charred
Salt and pepper to taste

1. Remove stems and seeds from chiles. Wash, then toast in a hot, dry pan about 10 seconds on each side.

2. In a saucepan, add half the oil and sauté the onion until translucent. Add garlic and sauté 1 minute. Add the remaining oil. Stir in the flour, coriander and cumin. Stir in the chicken stock and bring to a boil. Add the tomatoes to the mixture. Add the chiles. Turn heat down to simmer, cook for about 20 minutes. Add salt and pepper to taste.

3. Puree the sauce in a blender or food processor. Strain and adjust seasoning.

NOTE: This can be made ahead and frozen.

Chorizo (From Scratch)

2 pounds ground pork
6 cloves garlic, minced
2 tablespoons Mexican oregano
1 yellow onion, diced
½ teaspoon ground clove
1 teaspoon ground canela
1 teaspoon ground cumin
2 tablespoons pureed chipotle en adobo (optional)

If you can't purchase good-quality chorizo, use the following recipe.

1. Combine all ingredients and set aside until ready to use.

Stuffed Flank Steak with New Mexico Red Chile Sauce

SERVES 6

1½- to 2-pound flank steak
Sea salt and freshly ground
   black pepper

FILLING

2   tablespoons olive oil
1   medium red onion,
    diced
1   clove garlic, minced
1   medium red bell pepper,
    roasted, peeled, seeded
    and diced
½   cup frozen corn, thawed
½   cup cooked black beans
1   cup feta cheese,
    crumbled
1   egg, beaten with a fork
¼   teaspoon chipotle
    seasoning
½   teaspoon toasted and
    ground cumin seed
½   teaspoon salt
Freshly ground black pepper
   to taste
2   tablespoons vegetable or
    olive oil

1. Lay the steak out on a flat surface with the shortest side of the meat in front of you. The grain of the meat will be running north and south. Holding a long sharp knife (chef's, slicing or boning) horizontally, slice the steak in half making little slices through the center from one side to the other, until you reach one-half inch from the opposite side. Open the steak like a book, cover with a large piece of plastic wrap, and flatten with a meat pounder or mallet. Feel the surface with your hand and pound the steak to make sure it is evenly thick. Sprinkle the surface of the meat with a little salt and pepper. Set aside while you make the filling.

2. Heat the oil in a medium skillet over medium-high heat. Add the onion and sauté for 2 minutes, stirring occasionally. Add the garlic and cook 1 minute. Add the bell pepper, corn, beans and cheese and combine. Remove from the heat and stir in the egg, chipotle seasoning, cumin seed, salt and pepper to taste. Set aside.

3. With the grain of the meat running east and west, spread the filling on the beef to within an inch of the edges all the way around. Roll the meat up over the filling into a nice, tight roll. Secure the roll by tying kitchen string at 2-inch intervals around the rolled flank steak. Season the roll with salt and pepper on all sides.

4. Preheat the oven to 450° F. Position a rack one level up from the middle. Heat the oil in a large skillet over medium-high heat. Brown the steak roll on all sides and then move it to a foil-covered sheet pan. Roast the meat for 15 to 20 minutes, depending on the size of the roll, until the center is medium-rare to medium. If you cook this cut of meat too long, it will be tough.

5. When the meat is cooked, remove from the oven and let stand for 7 to 10 minutes so it can rest. Slice the meat into 1/2-inch-thick slices and serve with New Mexico Red Chile Sauce.

New Mexico Red Chile Sauce

YIELDS ABOUT 4 CUPS

8 Roma tomatoes

4 ounces dried New Mexico red chiles (about 15)

2 ounces dried ancho chiles (about 2 or 3)

2 ounces dried cascabel chiles (about 15)

1 tablespoon olive oil

1 white onion, peeled and diced

2 tablespoons pureed chipotles en adobo

1½ cups beef or chicken broth

3 large cloves roasted garlic, peeled and finely chopped

1 teaspoon freshly toasted ground cumin

2 teaspoons dried Mexican oregano

1 teaspoon salt

2 tablespoons lard or peanut oil

We always recommend reading a recipe all the way through before you begin your cooking process. This recipe is a perfect example of why we do this. The sauce calls for roasted garlic. Roasted garlic takes up to an hour to cook, so you want to have this done when you are ready to assemble the sauce.

1. Cut tomatoes in half lengthwise and place skin side up on a baking sheet. Broil until blackened, about 5 minutes.

2. Wash, stem and seed the chiles and place on a separate baking sheet. Bake at 250° F for 2 to 3 minutes. Shake occasionally and do not allow to blacken as the chiles will taste bitter. (Chiles can also be dry toasted in a single layer in a large heavy skillet over medium heat.) Transfer chiles to a large bowl and add enough boiling water to just cover. Allow to stand for 20 to 30 minutes until they are soft. Drain chiles and discard soaking liquid.

3. Heat the oil in a skillet and sauté onion over medium heat until well browned.

4. In a food processor or blender, puree all the ingredients, except the lard, to a fine paste, adding more broth or water if necessary.

5. Heat lard or oil in a heavy saucepan until just smoking. Fry the sauce for 3 to 5 minutes, stirring continuously. If the sauce becomes too thick, add more broth or water. Serve warm. This sauce will keep in the refrigerator for up to 1 week, and it freezes well.

Roasting Garlic Technique

Preheat the oven to 350° F. Cut off the top third from whole heads of garlic. You can save these pieces of garlic for soups and stews, or you can roast them along with the larger portions. Sprinkle the cut surfaces with olive oil, salt and pepper and wrap the heads in aluminum foil. Place the foil package in the oven and bake for 45 minutes to 1 hour, until the cloves are softened and golden. Let cool slightly. To remove the cloves, take a head, root end in the palm of your hand, and squeeze. If you just need a few individual cloves, you can peel and place in foil instead of whole heads. Although, you can keep roasted garlic in your refrigerator for up to 3 weeks in a sealed container.

Hearty Greens, Potato & Roasted Poblano Tacos

**YIELDS FILLING FOR
16 TO 20 TACOS**

4 poblano chiles
1 pound hearty greens
   (could be white or
   rainbow chard, kale,
   collards, or a
   combination)
1 tablespoon vegetable or
   olive oil
1 white onion, thinly
   sliced
3 cloves garlic, minced
¼ teaspoon fresh thyme
¼ teaspoon Mexican
   oregano
2 to 3 medium Yukon
   Gold potatoes, cubed
⅔ cup chicken broth, plus
   a bit more if needed
¾ cup crème fraîche or
   whipping cream
16 to 20 small corn tortillas
3 to 4 ounces crumbled
   queso fresco or ricotta
   salata for garnish

1. Roast the chiles on a Santa Fe School of Cooking grill until charred on all sides. Place in a paper or plastic bag to steam for 10 minutes. Peel the charred skin from the flesh of each chile and split the chiles down the side. Remove the stem and brush the seeds from the inside. Cut the chile flesh into 1/4-inch-wide strips and set aside.

2. Rinse the greens well to remove any dirt or sand and spin in a salad spinner or dry on paper towels. Trim out the thick center stem of each leaf and cut the leaves into 1/2-inch strips widthwise. Set aside.

3. Heat the oil in a large skillet over medium-high heat and sauté the onion until lightly browned but still a little crisp. Add the garlic and herbs and mix in the poblano strips. Set the skillet aside.

4. Combine the potatoes and the broth in a medium saucepan, cover and simmer for about 15 minutes, or until the potatoes are cooked but still a bit firm. Replace the skillet over medium-high heat and add the potatoes, greens and broth. Continue to simmer until the broth has evaporated. Add the crème fraîche and cook, stirring frequently, until the crème has thickened and coats the ingredients. Turn down the heat and keep the filling warm.

5. Warm the tortillas and fill each one with about 3 tablespoons of the filling. Garnish each taco with a bit of the crumbled cheese and serve.

Chipotle-Marinated Steak Fajitas with Chunky Avocado Salsa

SERVES 6

CHIPOTLE MARINADE

1	small white onion, peeled, cut into large pieces
6	cloves garlic, peeled
2	tablespoons toasted and ground coriander seeds
2	tablespoons toasted and ground cumin seeds
2	tablespoons pureed chipotles en adobo, or to taste
2	tablespoons dark brown sugar
2	tablespoons olive oil (optional)

Kosher salt to taste

STEAK FAJITAS

1½	pounds top round steak, trimmed of fat

Kosher salt to taste

Freshly ground black pepper to taste

Freshly squeezed lime juice

6	large, thin flour tortillas

Fajitas originated on the ranches in northern Mexico where the ranch hands were given the least popular part of the cattle to eat, the diaphragm muscle, known as skirt steak. The term is really misused today and generally embraces any marinated meat rolled in a flour tortilla. We like this recipe made with skirt steak; however, it can be a little difficult to find that cut of meat, so we recommend the top round or flank steak simply because they are easier to find.

FOR CHIPOTLE MARINADE

Pulse the onion and garlic in a food processor until finely chopped. Add the coriander, cumin, chipotles en adobo, brown sugar and oil, and pulse to combine thoroughly. The mixture should resemble a thick paste. Season with salt.

FOR FAJITAS

1. Rub steak with the Chipotle Marinade and set aside for at least 30 minutes.

2. Preheat grill. Season the meat with salt and pepper and sprinkle with lime juice. Grill to medium-rare over high heat, about 1 minute per side. Remove from the grill and cut into strips with the grain of the meat.

3. Lightly toast tortillas over a flame. Top tortillas with meat strips and serve with Chunky Avocado Salsa and other accompaniments.

TOASTING SPICES

To toast whole spices, place a small sauté pan with no oil over medium-high heat and add the desired amount of spice to the pan. Stir constantly until spices become very aromatic (a wisp of smoke may be seen). Remove from the pan and process in a suribachi, mortar and pestle or electric coffee grinder.

Chunky Avocado Salsa

3 ripe Roma tomatoes, diced

1 to 2 serrano chiles to taste, seeded and diced

Minced garlic (optional)

1 medium red onion, diced

¼ cup chopped fresh cilantro

3 large, ripe Haas avocados

Freshly squeezed lime juice to taste

Kosher salt to taste

This is just a slightly different version of guacamole. This dish needs to be made at the last minute. Ideally, don't let it stand for more than 30 minutes. After you have made it, press a piece of plastic wrap onto the surface of the dish. Ripe Haas avocados are the key ingredient!

1. Combine the tomatoes, chiles, garlic, onion and cilantro. Set aside.

2. Cut the avocados in half, running a knife around the pit from stem to blossom end and back again; twist the halves in opposite directions to free the pits and pull the halves apart. Cut each half into large chunks. Add to tomato mixture and stir gently to combine.

3. Season the salsa with lime juice and salt.

SPICE-RUBBED DUCK BREASTS

SERVES 6

SPICE RUB

6	tablespoons onion powder
4	tablespoons juniper berries, ground in a coffee grinder
4	tablespoons garlic powder
3	tablespoons kosher salt
2	tablespoons dried thyme leaves
2	tablespoons ground canela
2	tablespoons sugar
2	teaspoons toasted, ground coriander seed
2	teaspoons toasted, ground cumin seed
2	teaspoons chipotle seasoning
1	teaspoon ground allspice
1	teaspoon smoked paprika
6	(6- to 7-ounce) duck breasts, fat trimmed and scored
3	tablespoons extra virgin olive oil

There are three major duckling breeds available in the United States: White Pekin, Muscovy and Moulard. White Pekin has a mild flavor, tender texture and, although it has a layer of fat adjacent to the meat, contradicts the perception that duck is a fatty meat. These ducks are bred from select stock, chosen for leanness and raised on a highly nutritious diet with no hormones or artificial additives. Muscovy duck has a slightly more gamey flavor, and is also lean and meaty. Muscovy duck breasts are larger than the White Pekin variety. Muscovy ducks have less fat and calories per pound than turkey. Moulard ducks are most often used for foie gras. Wild duck is notorious for its tough meat and gamey flavor.

In this recipe, we use a White Pekin boneless duck breast from Maple Leaf Farms. It is available online, or in the freezer section of gourmet grocery stores.

TO PREPARE SPICE RUB

Combine all ingredients for the rub in a bowl and stir well to mix. Toss the duck breasts in 1/3 to 1/2 cup of the spice mix, using more if needed, to lightly coat on all sides.

NOTE: Leftover rub can be stored in a sealed container for up to 6 months.

TO PREPARE THE DUCK

1. Preheat the oven to 450° F and place a rack on the topmost position. Heat the oil in a nonstick skillet over medium-high heat. Add 3 duck breasts skin side down, and brown for 3 to 4 minutes, or until skin is a deep, golden brown. Turn breasts over and continue to sear for 2 minutes more.

2. Transfer the duck, skin side up, to a foil-covered baking sheet and sear the remaining breasts.

3. Place baking sheet in oven on top rack and roast the duck about 8 minutes for medium rare. Remove from oven and let the duck rest for at least 5 minutes so it will relax. Slice each breast on the diagonal and fan the slices to serve.

Santa Fe is surrounded by juniper trees, so it is only natural we would use the little purple berries the trees produce. Juniper berries have a woodsy fragrance and are often used in marinades, to make teas and most famously they are the hallmark flavoring of gin. They are too bitter to eat raw. Crush them to release their flavor. See photos of wildcrafting Juniper berries on page 97.

Lasagna with Ricotta Filling, Chipotle-Tomato Sauce & Poblano Pesto

SERVES 12

- **32 ounces whole milk ricotta cheese**
- **½ to 1 teaspoon freshly grated nutmeg to taste**
- **1 cup freshly grated Parmesan cheese**
- **½ to ¾ teaspoon kosher salt to taste**
- **¼ to ½ teaspoon freshly ground black or white pepper to taste**
- **12 "no boil" lasagna noodles (Barilla is a good brand)**
- **1¼ cups shredded mozzarella cheese (optional)**

Be sure to make your Poblano Pesto and Chipotle-Tomato Sauce ahead of time.

1. Preheat the oven to 400° F.

2. Mix the ricotta, nutmeg and cheese, and season with salt and pepper to taste. Set aside.

3. Brush the bottom of a 9 x 13-inch baking dish with a little extra virgin olive oil and spread 1 cup of the Chipotle-Tomato Sauce over the bottom of the dish. Place three of the noodles over the sauce, leaving a little space between them. Spread 1 cup of the ricotta mixture over the noodles. Repeat with sauce, noodles and ricotta twice more, ending with noodles and sauce. Cover the dish tightly with foil and bake on the middle shelf for 40 to 45 minutes. Remove the foil and sprinkle the top of the lasagna with mozzarella cheese. Bake, uncovered, for 15 minutes more, or until golden and bubbly. Remove the dish from the oven and let the lasagna stand for 10 minutes before cutting. Cut into 12 equal portions.

4. To serve, warm the remaining Chipotle-Tomato Sauce and ladle 4 tablespoons onto a dinner plate, spreading it out to cover the center. Place a portion of the lasagna in the middle of the plate and garnish with a spoonful of Poblano Pesto. Serve immediately.

SAUCE FROM FRESH TOMATOES VS. CANNED

When in season, there is nothing like fresh, locally grown tomatoes to produce an incredibly delicious sauce. But during winter months, canned tomatoes often can be more flavorful than what you can buy in the produce section of the grocery store. If using fresh tomatoes, cut them in half and grate them. Discard the skins and use the freshly grated tomatoes in equal portions to canned. One pound of fresh tomatoes should yield approximately 1 to 1 1/3 cups grated tomatoes.

CHIPOTLE-TOMATO SAUCE

3   tablespoons extra virgin
    olive oil
1   medium white onion, finely
    chopped
3   cloves garlic, minced
1   28-ounce can whole Italian
    Roma tomatoes with juice
1   15-ounce can diced tomatoes
    with juice
2   teaspoons Mexican oregano
2   teaspoons toasted ground
    coriander seed
2   teaspoons toasted ground
    cumin seed
2   teaspoons chipotle
    seasoning, or more to taste
½   to ¾ teaspoon kosher salt to
    taste
1   to 2 teaspoons sugar to taste

Heat the oil in a heavy saucepan over medium heat and add the onion. Cook for 5 minutes, stirring frequently, until the onion is soft and translucent. Add the garlic and continue cooking another 2 minutes. Add the tomatoes and bring the mixture to a boil. Reduce the heat, stir in the oregano, coriander, cumin, chipotle seasoning, salt and sugar. Simmer the mixture for 20 minutes, or until the sauce has thickened slightly. Remove from the heat and cool for 10 minutes.

POBLANO PESTO

½   pound tomatillos
8   tablespoons olive oil, divided
Kosher salt and pepper to taste
6   cloves garlic, peeled
2   tablespoons New Mexico
    piñon, or other pine nuts
4   poblano chiles, roasted,
    peeled, seeded, with stems
    removed
Salt to taste
Fresh lime juice or juice from
    pickled jalapeños to taste

1. Preheat the oven to 400° F.

2. Soak the tomatillos for 10 minutes in hot water. Remove the outer papery husk and pat the tomatillos dry with paper towels. Toss them with 2 tablespoons oil, and sprinkle with salt and pepper. Place on a baking sheet and roast in the oven for 20 minutes, or until soft and lightly browned. Cool.

3. Place the garlic in a small skillet with 2 tablespoons oil over medium heat. Sauté until cloves are lightly browned and set aside.

4. Place the garlic and piñon nuts in the work bowl of a food processor and finely chop. Add the tomatillos and their juice, the poblano chiles and remaining oil and puree until smooth. Season with salt and lime juice to taste. Make sure the puree is thin enough to drizzle, adding 1 or 2 tablespoons water if it seems too thick. Pour the mixture into a container, cover with plastic wrap pressed onto the surface of the pesto and set aside.

Pollo Tacos in Salsa Verde

SERVES 8 TO 10

TACO FILLING

¾ pound fresh tomatillos (about 8), husked and rinsed under hot water for 30 seconds

3 tablespoons vegetable oil, divided

½ white onion, chopped

1 or 2 fresh jalapeños, stemmed and sliced

4 cloves garlic, peeled

½ teaspoon salt

1 teaspoon granulated sugar

2 teaspoons chopped fresh epazote or marjoram (or 1 teaspoon toasted dried Mexican oregano)

1 teaspoon apple cider vinegar or rice wine vinegar

½ cup water

2 or 3 chiles de arbol or other small dry red chiles, toasted, stemmed and seeds removed

2 pounds (about 8 to 10 pieces) boneless chicken thighs, cut into 1-inch square pieces

1 teaspoon Chimayo chile powder (optional)

Salt and pepper to taste

TACOS

Corn tortillas

1 cup grated asadero or Monterey Jack cheese

1. Roast the tomatillos on a Santa Fe School of Cooking grill, or in a hot oven using the broiler, until about half the surfaces are well charred.

2. In a preheated skillet or heavy saucepan, add 1 tablespoon oil, onion, jalapeños and garlic; sauté until onion is slightly browned and beginning to soften.

3. Place in a blender with roasted tomatillos, salt, sugar, herbs, vinegar, water and dry chiles. Puree until smooth.

4. In the same skillet or pan, add remaining oil and heat until just beginning to smoke (very hot). Season chicken pieces with chile powder, salt and pepper; cook until browned on all sides.

5. Pour in puree, stir well, and reduce heat to simmer. Cook, stirring occasionally, for about 10 to 12 minutes. Remove from heat. Sauce should be fairly thick.

6. Place corn tortillas on a baking sheet, top with chicken mixture and about a teaspoon of grated cheese. Place under a broiler or in a very hot oven (475° F) until heated through and cheese has melted.

CHILE CON CARNE

SERVES 8

1 heaping cup diced onion

4 tablespoons fat (olive oil, vegetable oil, butter or lard)

4 teaspoons chopped garlic

3 pounds stew meat (beef, venison, lamb, pork or a combination) cut into ½-inch dice

Salt

¼ cup mild Chimayo chile powder

¼ cup medium Chimayo chile powder

2 ancho chiles, soaked in hot water, stems and seeds removed, then diced

2 tablespoons Mexican oregano

1 tablespoon freshly ground cumin

¼ cup brown sugar

1 quart, more or less, water, meat broth or chicken broth

1 tablespoon salt

1 small can diced tomatoes (optional)

4 tablespoons masa harina

CONDIMENTS

Sliced, pickled jalapeños or fresh chopped chiles

Chile caribe

Hot sauce

Sour cream

Salt

Lime wedges

Fresh radishes

Shredded cheddar and Monterey Jack cheese

Diced red onion or sliced green onion

If we were really being accurate, we would be spelling this dish "chili con carne," since this is the traditional Texas recipe, but Texans and New Mexicans have never agreed on the correct spelling of chile. In New Mexico, we only spell it with the e on the end. However, in Texas, they use the e on the end when referring to the capsicum plant and its pods and the i on the end when referring to this dish or other related products. This is another contribution from our Texan, Allen Smith.

1. Sauté onion into the fat until it starts to soften. Add the garlic and sauté 30 seconds. Add the meat, season generously with salt and sear.

2. Add the rest of the ingredients except masa harina.

3. Bring to a boil, stir, reduce heat to a simmer. Simmer, partially covered, stirring occasionally for 45 minutes to 1 hour, or until the meat is tender.

4. Blend the masa harina with a little water and pour about half the mixture into the chile, bring back to a boil and reduce to a simmer. After several minutes the chile broth should be slightly thickened. If it isn't, add a bit more of the masa mixture and repeat the procedure.

5. Taste for seasoning. Skim some of the fat, if desired. The flavor of the chile will improve if allowed to sit overnight.

6. Serve with some or all of the condiments for cooling it down or heating it up.

Southwestern Chicken Breasts with Pan Applesauce

SERVES 6

3 whole skinless, boneless chicken breasts

FILLING

6 ounces soft goat cheese or goat ricotta

2 teaspoons fresh thyme leaves

1½ teaspoons chipotles en adobo

COATING

1 cup all-purpose flour

1½ teaspoons kosher salt

½ teaspoon freshly ground black pepper

2 eggs

¾ cup milk

1¼ cups bread crumbs

½ cup finely chopped pecans

1 tablespoon pure, ground Chimayo red chile

1 tablespoon lemon zest, finely chopped

Steve Cooper created this recipe for a restaurant owned by a soap opera star whose style was coined "genteel American home cooking." This became one of the most popular items on the menu! He shared it with us, but, of course, we Southwesternized it by adding some chile!

1. Preheat the oven to 375° F.

2. Separate the chicken breasts by cutting down both sides of the center bit of gristle. Discard the gristle. Pull aside the tenderloin from the center and find the depression at the base of the thickest part of the breast. Insert a sharp knife and gently cut a pocket. If you pivot the knife at the entry point, you will be able to leave an opening that will hold the filling while cooking.

3. Mix the goat cheese, thyme and chipotle. Stuff the opening in the chicken breast with 1 1/2 to 2 tablespoons of the mixture, pressing it inside the opening with your fingers. Fold the tenderloin over the hole to seal. At this point you may refrigerate for later use or continue.

4. For the coating, combine the flour, salt and pepper, whisking thoroughly to combine. In a separate bowl, beat the eggs with the milk. In a third bowl, mix the crumbs, pecans, chile and lemon zest. Dredge the chicken breasts first in the flour, then the eggwash, and then coat with the crumb mixture and set aside for about 5 minutes.

5. Cover a baking sheet with aluminum foil. Place the stuffed chicken breasts on the sheet and bake for about 15 to 20 minutes. If the breasts are large they may take 5 to 10 minutes longer. Serve with Pan Applesauce.

Pan Applesauce

4   medium apples, peeled,
    cored and sliced into
    ¼-inch slices
1   cup orange juice
1   teaspoon ground canela
¼   teaspoon ground
    nutmeg
2   tablespoons brown sugar
Pinch of salt

1. Combine all the ingredients in a saucepan or skillet and simmer, stirring occasionally, until the apples are tender, about 20 minutes. If you need to add a bit more orange juice to keep the mixture moist, do. New Mexico winesaps are perfect for this recipe, but you must use 6 to 8 of them because they are small.

Seafood Brochettes with Toasted Fennel Seed Vinaigrette

SERVES 6

6   wooden skewers, about 8 inches long

1½ pounds firm fresh fish (sword, tuna, marlin, salmon, etc.), cut into 1-inch cubes

12 large shrimp, peeled and deveined

2   to 3 tablespoons olive oil

1   tablespoon crushed Mexican oregano

Kosher salt and freshly ground black pepper to taste

1. Soak skewers in water to prevent them from burning on the grill.

2. Place the fish cubes and shrimp in a medium bowl and toss with oil, oregano, salt and pepper.

3. Alternately thread three cubes of fish and 2 shrimp on each skewer (fish-shrimp-fish-shrimp-fish). Sear in a dry, nonstick pan, or grill for about 2 to 4 minutes per side until cooked to satisfaction. Serve dressed with a spoonful of Toasted Fennel Seed Vinaigrette over each brochette.

> **GRAPESEED OIL**
> Grapeseed oil is the byproduct of wine production, making it an ecologically good agricultural product. The slightly nutty flavor, high smoking point (485° F) and reported health benefits make grapeseed oil an excellent cooking oil.

Toasted Fennel Seed Vinaigrette

1   clove garlic, minced

1   tablespoon capers, minced

2   teaspoons whole grain mustard

2   teaspoons chopped fresh tarragon

1   teaspoon whole fennel seed, toasted and crushed

1   teaspoon chile caribe

3   tablespoons fresh lemon juice

3   tablespoons white wine vinegar

3   teaspoons sugar

⅔ cup grapeseed or olive oil

Kosher salt and freshly ground black pepper to taste

Mix together all the ingredients except the oil. Slowly whisk in the oil and season to taste with salt and pepper. Set aside.

Rocky's New Mexican Pot Roast

SERVES 6 TO 8

5   **pounds rump roast**
1   **tablespoon salt**
¼   **cup flour**
¼   **cup Chimayo chile powder**
1   **tablespoon black pepper**
2   **to 3 tablespoons oil for searing**
2   **yellow onions, diced**
3   **celery ribs, diced**
3   **baking potatoes, large, diced**

Wine for deglazing

4   **to 6 cloves garlic, peeled and crushed**
4   **to 6 sprigs fresh thyme**
1   **10-ounce can crushed tomatoes**
3   **cups beef, chicken or vegetable stock**
1   **to 1½ cups hearty red wine**

This chile-seasoned pot roast takes quite a while to cook. We recommend making the entire recipe even if you are feeding fewer than 6. What you don't eat the first day just gets better the second.

1. Season beef on all sides with salt. Combine flour, chile and black pepper and then dredge beef in dry mixture.

2. Heat oil in a large, heavy-bottomed, oven-safe pan and sear meat on all sides and then remove from pan. Add vegetables to the pan and sauté for 8 to 10 minutes, stirring occasionally. Deglaze pan with wine and simmer for 3 to 4 minutes. Add remaining ingredients and return beef to pan. Cover and place in an oven preheated to 375° F. Cook for 3 1/2 to 4 1/2 hours or until beef is fork tender. (To speed up cooking, the roast can be cut into two equal pieces before being dredged and seared.)

3. Cut roast against the grain in thick slices. The slices may be cut into 3 or 4 pieces. Serve meat and vegetables with braising sauce spooned over the top.

To deglaze, bring the mixture to a simmer and scrape the bottom and sides of the pan incorporating the browned particles in the liquid mixture.

Brazilian Kabobs with Vinaigrette Salsa

**SERVES 6 AS AN ENTRÉE
OR 12 AS AN APPETIZER**

Wooden skewers (as many as
    needed)
1   onion, diced
¼   cup sugar
8   cloves garlic
½   cup sherry vinegar
2   tablespoons salt
1   tablespoon black pepper
1   cup olive oil
2   pounds beef sirloin or
    tenderloin
1   pound thinly sliced
    bacon

1. Soak skewers in water to prevent them from burning on the grill.

2. In a blender or food processor, place onion, sugar, garlic, vinegar, salt and pepper and puree. Stir in oil.

3. Cut beef into 1/2-inch cubes. Pour puree over cubes and marinate for at least 2 hours.

4. Cut strips of bacon in half and wrap around each cube of beef and place on skewer.

5. Grill or sauté until done. Serve with Vinaigrette Salsa.

Vinaigrette Salsa

½   cup diced red bell
    pepper
½   cup diced green bell
    pepper
½   cup diced red onion
1   cup diced tomato
¼   cup sherry vinegar
2   tablespoons olive oil
1   tablespoon Mexican
    oregano
2   teaspoons coriander,
    toasted and ground
Salt and pepper to taste

Combine all ingredients in a bowl and mix well.

Grilled Eggplant "Enchiladas" with Red Chile Sauce

SERVES 6

RED CHILE SAUCE

½ cup Chimayo chile powder

8 to 10 blackened tomatoes (roast in oven or over direct flame until charred)

3 cloves garlic, chopped and sautéed until lightly browned

½ teaspoon cumin seed, toasted and ground (see toasting herbs p. 144)

½ teaspoon coriander seed, toasted and ground

1 teaspoon toasted Mexican oregano (optional)

1½ to 2 cups chicken or vegetable stock

1 tablespoon honey (optional)

Salt and pepper to taste

1 cup New Mexican goat cheese, feta, or ricotta cheese, crumbled

1 cup grated cheddar or Monterey Jack cheese

2 eggplants, sliced ¼ inch thick, lightly oiled and grilled, or broiled

1 large onion, diced and sautéed until golden

A version of this was developed by Rocky Durham for our Low-Carb Southwest class.

1. Place all sauce ingredients in a blender and puree.

2. Mix cheeses together.

3. Pour 1/3 of red chile sauce on the bottom of an oven-safe dish. Arrange 1/3 of the eggplant slices over sauce. Cover with 1/3 of the sautéed onion, then 1/3 of cheese mixture. Continue the layers two more times, ending with a cheese layer on top.

3. Bake in an oven at 350° F until cheeses are melted and top is slightly brown, about 15 to 18 minutes.

Rather than layering this dish, you can make individual, rolled enchiladas. Place 3 tablespoons of cheese mixture in middle of eggplant, place all rolled eggplant in dish, cover with red chile sauce and bake.

Eggplant comes in a variety of colors. Is there a difference? Yes! Generally speaking, the lighter the color, the milder the flavor. Those great-looking red-orange eggplants are actually quite bitter and best to be used for pickling. Also, the long varieties seem to be milder than the round ones. Eggplant can be visually stunning and people tend to want to leave it out on the counter, but it really stores best in a cool place and ideally should be used within a couple of days.

Paella Carnaval

SERVES 10 TO 12

1	pound bacon, diced
1	medium onion, diced
2	red bell peppers, diced
2	green bell peppers, diced
2	jalapeños, chopped
8	tomatoes, diced
6	cloves garlic, chopped
1	pound andouille sausage sliced 1 inch thick
1	pound chicken breast, cut in pieces
4	tablespoons smoked paprika
4	cups chicken stock
2	cups Uncle Ben's par-boiled rice
½	pound shrimp, peeled and deveined
1	pound mussels
1	pound frozen green peas

This recipe is really a combination of New Orleans–style gumbo and Spanish paella. This dish is easy to prepare. People always complain about getting the rice done enough when cooking paella. Using Uncle Ben's par-boiled rice is a good trick to making sure that the rice is ready when everything else is.

1. In a Dutch oven or paella pan, cook bacon over medium heat to release fat.

2. Remove the bacon with a slotted spoon and set aside. Add the onion, peppers, jalapeños, tomatoes and garlic to the bacon grease and cook for 10 minutes. Add the sausage and chicken. Stir in paprika. Cook for 10 minutes more. Add chicken stock and rice, let cook for 25 minutes, or until rice is tender.

3. During the last 10 minutes of cooking, add the shrimp, cooked bacon and mussels.

4. Add frozen peas at the end of cooking so they don't dry out.

Piñon Apple Tart

Sweet Coconut Rice Pudding

Amaretto Chocolate Mousse

Dixon Apple Pie Tamales

New Mexico Piñon Shortbread

Desserts

Piñon Apple Tart

SERVES 12

CRUST

1   **cup all-purpose flour**

1   **teaspoon sugar**

Pinch of salt

½   **cup (1 stick) chilled unsalted butter, cut into ¼-inch slices**

¼   **teaspoon Mexican vanilla**

1   **tablespoon ice water or more if needed**

FILLING

1¼   **cups heavy cream**

½   **cup sugar**

Pinch of salt

2   **tablespoons calvados or domestic apple brandy**

1   **cup dried apples, cut into ½-inch pieces (packed)**

1   **cup toasted New Mexico piñon nuts**

½   **teaspoon Mexican vanilla**

Whipped cream, optional

FOR THE CRUST

1. Pulse the flour, sugar and salt in a food processor to mix. Add the butter and process to the size of bread crumbs. Add the vanilla and cold water, and pulse until the mixture just comes together, adding more water if needed. Turn the dough onto a sheet of plastic wrap, flatten into a circle, wrap in the plastic and refrigerate for at least 1 hour.

2. On a lightly floured surface, roll the dough to a thickness of about 1/4 to 1/8 inch. This dough is very tender, so work with it while it is cool to avoid tearing. Carefully fold in quarters and place in a 9-inch tart pan with a removable bottom. Unfold the dough and press it evenly over the bottom and up the sides of the pan. Trim the dough from the top edge. Place the tart pan in the freezer and chill for 30 minutes.

3. Preheat the oven to 400° F. Place a piece of foil large enough to line the tart shell over the dough and press it onto the dough. Add rice, beans or pie weights to the foil and distribute evenly. Bake the tart shell for 20 minutes, until it begins to set and turn golden. Remove the shell from the oven and cool slightly. Remove the foil and weights. Reduce the temperature to 350° F.

FOR THE FILLING

1. In a heavy saucepan, mix the cream, sugar, salt, calvados and apples. Cook the mixture over low heat until the sugar has dissolved and the texture is silky, 10 to 15 minutes. Stir in the piñon nuts and vanilla. Cool mixture slightly and pour into the tart shell.

2. Place tart on a foil-lined baking sheet and bake on the center rack for about 30 minutes. The filling may bubble up and overflow, but will settle and begin to caramelize. Rotate the tart frequently during the last 15 minutes of baking so the top is an even deep golden brown.

3. Remove tart to a rack and cool to room temperature before cutting. Serve with unsweetened whipped cream, if desired.

Sweet Coconut Rice Pudding

SERVES 8

2   15-ounce cans
    unsweetened coconut
    milk
3   cups milk
1   1-inch long piece peeled
    ginger
3   sticks canela
3   strips lemon or orange
    zest
¾   cups arborio rice
Pinch of salt
⅓   to ½ cup sugar
1   teaspoon Mexican
    vanilla
1   teaspoon orange flower
    water
**Orange slices or segments
    (optional)**
Toasted almonds (optional)
Toasted coconut (optional)

1. Combine the milks, ginger, canela and zest in a large saucepan, and bring to a boil. Stir in the rice, salt and sugar. Reduce heat to low and simmer the mixture, stirring occasionally, for about 1 hour, or until it has thickened.

2. Remove pan from the heat and cool to room temperature. Remove the ginger, canela sticks and zest, and stir in the vanilla and orange flower water. Garnish individual servings with oranges, almonds and/or coconut, as desired.

James Campbell developed this recipe for our New World Tapas class. A version of this recipe can be found in his book, *El Farol: Tapas and Spanish Cuisine.*

Canela is the flaky bark of a tree native to Sri Lanka and southwestern India that produces what some would argue is true cinnamon. Nobody in Mexico, or here at the cooking school for that matter, would ever consider using the hard-barked cassia that often passes for cinnamon in the United States. It is less aromatic, more difficult to grind and has a slightly bitter aftertaste. If you can't find canela, you can use regular store-bought cinnamon, but use slightly less. Canela comes in sticks and must be ground for use.

Anise Pound Cake

SERVES 10 TO 12

1   cup (2 sticks) unsalted
    butter, at room
    temperature
8   ounces cream cheese, at
    room temperature
1⅓ cups sugar
3   large eggs
3   large egg yolks
1½ teaspoons anise extract
1½ teaspoons Mexican
    vanilla
2   cups all-purpose flour
1½ teaspoons baking
    powder
Pinch of salt
2   teaspoons toasted
    ground anise seed
Grated zest of 2 lemons

1. Preheat the oven to 325° F. Adjust a rack to center position. Coat a 9 x 5 x 3 1/2-inch loaf pan (7 1/2-cup) with vegetable cooking spray.

2. With a hand mixer on medium-high, beat butter until smooth and shiny, about 15 seconds. Cut the cream cheese into chunks and add to the butter. Continue to beat until fluffy. With the mixer still running, slowly sprinkle in sugar. Beat until almost white, 3 to 4 minutes, stopping to scrape the sides of the bowl.

3. Mix eggs, yolks and extracts in a glass measuring cup and set into a pan of warm water until the mixture reaches room temperature. With mixer at medium-high, take 3 to 5 minutes to add the egg mixture to the butter/sugar mixture in a very slow, thin stream.

4. Whisk the flour, baking powder, salt and anise seed together. Sprinkle 1/2 cup of the flour mixture over batter and fold in. Gently repeat the process, 1/2 cup of flour at a time. Fold in the lemon zest. Scrape the batter into the prepared pan and smooth the top. Bake until a cake tester comes out clean, 60 to 80 minutes. Let the cake rest 5 minutes and invert onto a wire rack. Then invert again. Cool and serve with fruit puree, sprinkled with powdered sugar, or whipped cream.

FLOURLESS CHOCOLATE TORTE

SERVES 10 TO 12

14 ounces semisweet
 chocolate
1¼ cups (2½ sticks)
 unsalted butter
8 large eggs, separated
½ cup sugar, divided
1 cup piñon nuts, ground
1 teaspoon vanilla paste

The beautiful design on this dessert can be made by cutting out the shape or shapes of your choice on a sheet of paper, set it on top of the torte and sprinkle with powdered sugar!

1. Preheat oven to 350° F.

2. Melt chocolate and butter together over a double boiler. Once melted, let cool for 15 minutes. Whisk together yolks with half the sugar until light and lemony in color. Slowly add the chocolate to the yolks, stirring constantly. Add the nuts.

3. Whisk egg whites with remaining sugar until stiff peaks are achieved. Fold half the whites into chocolate mixture. Then fold in remaining whites.

4. Pour into a springform pan with buttered sides and parchment lining the bottom.

5. Place pan in oven and bake for 25 to 30 minutes, or until a wooden skewer inserted in the middle comes out clean.

6. Cool cake before decorating with powdered sugar.

NOTE: If the cake isn't smooth on the top after baking, turn it upside down for an even surface for decorating.

PRICKLY PEAR SYRUP
Lois Ellen Frank, our instructor who specializes in Native American cuisine, introduced us to this fabulous product! It is one of those little secrets you will be glad to know about. Prickly pear syrup is a gorgeous magenta color and is quite tasty and sweet. It is made from the tuna, which is the greenish-yellow, egg-sized fruit of the cactus. It has a bright red flesh and tastes slightly of sour cherries. Keep some in a squirt bottle in your refrigerator, and when you are plating desserts, squirt some on the bottom of the plate. It makes the dessert look like it came out of a five-star restaurant kitchen! It works best with cakes, tortes and flans. The syrup can also be used in lemonade, margaritas or as a glaze on ham.

Key Lime Tart

SERVES 8 TO 10

CRUST

1¾ cups graham cracker crumbs

2 tablespoons sugar

Pinch of salt

2 teaspoons ground canela

½ cup (1 stick) unsalted butter, melted

FILLING

1½ tablespoons grated lime zest

4 large egg yolks

2 14-ounce cans sweetened condensed milk

¾ cup fresh lime juice

GARNISH

¾ cup lightly whipped cream

1 lime, sliced paper thin

FOR THE CRUST

1. Adjust an oven rack to center position and preheat the oven to 350° F. Mix the crumbs, sugar, salt and canela in a medium bowl. Add the butter and stir with a fork until well blended. Press the mixture evenly over the bottom and about 1 to 1 1/2 inches up the sides of a 9-inch springform pan. Bake until lightly browned and fragrant, about 8 to 10 minutes.

FOR THE FILLING

1. Whisk the zest and yolks in a medium bowl and let stand 2 minutes. Whisk in the condensed milk and lime juice and set aside to thicken at room temperature. This will happen almost immediately.

2. Pour filling into the crust and bake until the center is set, about 20 minutes. Cool to room temperature and refrigerate until well chilled, at least 3 hours.

3. Serve with whipped cream and garnish with lime slices.

Pecan-Rum-Raisin Cake

SERVES 10

2 cups raisins

¾ cup dark rum, divided

¼ cup water

1½ cups chopped pecan pieces

¼ cup honey

¼ cup sour cream

4 cups unbleached all-purpose flour

2½ teaspoons baking powder

1½ teaspoons baking soda

1¼ cups (2½ sticks) unsalted butter, at room temperature

1½ cups packed brown sugar

2 teaspoons Mexican vanilla

1 teaspoon salt

5 large eggs, at room temperature

GLAZE

4 tablespoons unsalted butter

½ cup sugar

2 tablespoons water

⅓ cup dark rum

1. Preheat the oven to 325° F. Thoroughly butter a large Bundt pan.

2. Combine raisins, 1/2 cup rum and water in a small saucepan. Cook over low, stirring frequently, until the liquid is absorbed. Set aside to cool. Stir in the chopped pecans.

3. In a small bowl, combine the honey and sour cream. Add remaining rum and reserve. In another bowl, stir together the flour, baking powder and baking soda.

4. With an electric mixer, cream together butter and brown sugar until light and fluffy. Beat in vanilla and salt. Add eggs, one at a time, beating well on medium after each addition.

5. Add the flour mixture, alternating with the sour cream/honey mixture, mixing gently between additions, ending with liquid. Fold in the rum-soaked raisins and nuts.

6. Spoon the batter evenly into the prepared pan. Smooth the top with a spatula and tap the pan on the counter to release air bubbles. Bake for 60 to 75 minutes, until a skewer inserted in the center comes out dry. Cool on a rack.

7. Poke a few deep holes in the cake with a skewer and brush on 1/3 of the glaze. Turn the cake out of the pan onto a baking sheet and brush remaining glaze over the top and sides of the cake. Let cool completely before serving.

FOR GLAZE

1. Combine butter, sugar and water in a small saucepan, bring to a boil and boil for 2 minutes. Remove from heat and stir in rum.

Dixon Apple Pie Tamales

SERVES 6

2   **eggs plus 1 yolk**

½   **cup brown sugar**

¾   **cup heavy cream**

1   **loaf French bread, cubed**

6   **Dixon or tart cooking apples, peeled and diced**

¼   **cup plus 1 tablespoon brown sugar**

1   **teaspoon ground canela**

1   **tablespoon corn starch**

3   **tablespoons sour cream**

6   **to 8 corn husks, soaked and drained**

1. Mix eggs, yolk, sugar and cream until sugar is dissolved. Add cubed bread and toss until well soaked.

2. Toss apples, sugar, canela, corn starch and sour cream.

3. Combine and mix the bread and apple mixtures.

4. Place in a parchment-lined pan and bake at 350° F for 50 to 60 minutes. Turn onto work surface and cut into rectangles 1 1/2 inch by 3 inches. Place in husk and garnish with powdered sugar, or Crème Anglaise (see page 183).

The Story of Mexican Vanilla

Vanilla is currently produced in Indonesia, Bali, Tonga, Tahiti, the Bourbon Islands (Madagascar is one of them) and Mexico. However, vanilla originated in Mexico. Vanilla pods or beans are the fruit of an orchid. Of the thousands of varieties of the orchid, the vanilla plant is the only one with an edible fruit. Because of its shape, the orchid needs assistance to be pollinated in order to produce a pod. Originally, this was done by a tiny bee found only in Mexico. For over 300 years after its discovery by Europeans, vanilla pods were produced only in Mexico because of this bee.

Eventually, it was discovered that it could not become fertilized without aid and a method of fertilizing by hand was developed; this method is still in use today. Each vanilla flower opens for only part of one day and if not pollinated on that day, no pod will be produced. Fortunately, the flowers do not all open on the same day but over a period of about two months. Each vine has to be visited every day to check on the condition of the flowering. Six to nine months after pollination, the yellowish-green pods are picked and the curing process begins. The characteristic vanilla flavor and aroma are not present in the green pods.

In Mexico, the vanilla beans are wrapped in blankets and placed in ovens for 24 to 48 hours. From this point on, the beans are brown in color. The purpose of these steps is to kill the beans and stop their ripening. About five pounds of green, uncured beans are required to make one pound of properly cured beans.

Many people comment that they can buy inexpensive vanilla in Mexico. However, as is obvious from the description of producing vanilla, it is not an inexpensive product. Unfortunately, there are many companies manufacturing vanilla in Mexico and labeling it as "pure" when, in fact, it is imitation vanilla. There is not an effective Food and Drug Administration overseeing their operations. Any ingredient can be used and labeled as "pure" vanilla. The basic flavor ingredients of most imitation vanillas is Vanillin. Most Vanillin is an artificial product derived from a by-product of the paper industry. The price charged for these imitation vanillas is normally extremely low, making it seem like a bargain.

What makes Mexican vanilla different from vanilla from Madagascar? Vanilla beans grown in various parts of the world all have slightly different flavor tones. The soil and curing variances produce subtle flavor differences. Some will certainly argue that Mexican vanilla is truly the finest. Unfortunately, only 10 percent of the world's vanilla is from Mexico these days. Mexican vanilla bean production has declined because the same area has oil fields and orange groves, both of which are more convenient and profitable than the labor-intensive vanilla bean.

At the Santa Fe School of Cooking, we use only pure vanilla from Nielsen-Massey Vanilla, Inc. They have built a reputation for the quality of their pure vanillas. They manufacture their vanillas from beans imported from Mexico and other places.

In recent years, Nielson-Massey has developed a vanilla bean paste using a cold extraction process that removes all the flavor components from the vanilla bean. This yields a highly aromatic, flavorful liquid that is infused into an all-natural base. The thick gel suspends the characteristic vanilla bean seeds, which are the source of the vanilla's signature flavor. The seeds and paste texture give desserts a gourmet look without the effort of scraping the seeds from the whole vanilla bean.

In using vanilla extract, vanilla paste and vanilla beans, substitutions are:

> *Vanilla extract and vanilla paste: Equal measurements*
>
> *One vanilla bean is equal to 1 tablespoon of paste or extract*

Amaretto Chocolate Mousse

SERVES 6

4 ounces bittersweet chocolate, coarsely chopped

4 ounces semisweet chocolate, coarsely chopped

4 ounces Ibarra Mexican chocolate, coarsely chopped

2 eggs

2 tablespoons brown sugar

2 teaspoons Mexican vanilla

2 teaspoons amaretto

Pinch of salt

1½ cups heavy cream (or half-and-half)

This is a popular dessert here because it is so tasty and so easy!

1. In a blender, mix all ingredients except cream for 30 seconds.

2. Heat cream until it just reaches the boiling point. With the blender running, pour in hot cream and blend for 1 minute.

3. Pour the mixture into individual ramekins. Refrigerate until set, approximately 30 minutes.

In Mexico, the cocoa beans used in Mexican chocolate are toasted very dark to give it an unusual flavor, then ground over heat with different spices, which are often some combination of sugar, canela, almonds and vanilla. It is not heavily beaten and is quite grainy with a coarse texture. Some Mexican chocolate such as Ibarra and Mayordomo is imported into the United States. However, if you can't find any, you can substitute 1 ounce semi-sweet chocolate, 1/2 teaspoon ground cinnamon, and 1 drop almond extract for 1 ounce Mexican chocolate.

Coconut Pound Cake

SERVES 8 TO 10

½ cup (1 stick) unsalted butter, at room temperature

1 cup granulated sugar

2 large eggs

2 teaspoons coconut extract

2 teaspoons Mexican vanilla

1 cup sour cream

1 cup sweetened flaked coconut

2 cups all-purpose flour

1 teaspoon baking powder

1 teaspoon baking soda

¼ teaspoon salt

1. Preheat oven to 350° F. Lightly butter an 8 x 4 x 2 3/4-inch loaf pan.

2. Cream butter and sugar. Beat in eggs, one at a time, extracts, sour cream and coconut. Combine flour, baking powder, baking soda and salt, and fold into butter mixture.

3. Spoon batter into prepared pan and bake in the center of the oven for 45 to 55 minutes, or until a toothpick comes out clean.

4. Cool the finished loaf on a rack for 15 minutes; turn out onto a rack and continue cooling.

NOTE: Cake may be made 1 day ahead and kept in an airtight container or wrapped in plastic wrap at room temperature.

STRAWBERRY TEQUILA MOUSSE

SERVES 6

8   **ounces fresh strawberries, rinsed and hulled**

LIME CURD

5   **large eggs**

½   **cup sugar**

½   **cup freshly squeezed lime juice**

Pinch of salt

1   **to 2 tablespoons gold or white tequila to taste**

1   **to 2 tablespoons triple sec to taste (optional)**

¾   **cup heavy whipping cream**

Fresh strawberries and mint sprigs for garnish

Puree the strawberries in a food processor or blender. Yield should be approximately 1 cup. Set aside.

TO MAKE THE LIME CURD

1. Whisk the eggs, sugar, lime juice and salt in a medium bowl. Pour the mixture into a medium saucepan and cook over low heat, stirring constantly, until thickened, 6 to 8 minutes. Immediately strain the curd through a fine-mesh sieve into a clean bowl. Stir in the strawberry puree, tequila and triple sec, if using, and chill the mixture for 1 hour.

1. Whip the cream to soft peaks and fold into the mousse. Refrigerate until ready to serve.

2. Garnish each serving with a fresh strawberry and a mint sprig.

Pink Grapefruit–Tequila Sorbet

YIELDS 1 QUART (16 ¼-CUP SERVINGS)

4   cups freshly squeezed pink grapefruit juice (5 to 6 grapefruit)

⅓   cup sugar

1   to 2 tablespoons Campari (optional)

¼   cup gold tequila

This is a light, refreshing finish to a spicy meal. Have your equipment already to go prior to starting this recipe, and read the manufacturer's instructions. Some ice cream machines require the bowls frozen before use.

Mix the juice and sugar and Campari, if using, in a pitcher and stir until the sugar has dissolved. Pour through a fine-mesh sieve and chill for 1 hour in the refrigerator. Freeze in an ice cream machine according to manufacturer's instructions. As alcohol inhibits the freezing process, add the tequila when the mixture is semi-stiff.

New Mexico Piñon Shortbread

YIELDS ABOUT 30 COOKIES

½   cup toasted New Mexico piñon nuts (pine nuts may be substituted)

2   cups unbleached all-purpose flour

½   cup sugar

2   teaspoons freshly ground canela (cinnamon may be substituted)

Pinch of kosher salt

1   cup (2 sticks) unsalted butter, chilled and cut into tablespoon-sized pieces

1. Place the piñon nuts in a dry pan on medium heat and lightly brown. Allow to cool. Pulse the nuts in a food processor until coarsely chopped. Remove and set aside. In the work bowl of the food processor, combine the flour, sugar, canela and salt. Pulse about 10 times to mix. Return the nuts to the work bowl. Add the butter and pulse until the mixture just begins to form a ball. At this point the dough may be wrapped and refrigerated for up to 2 days. A chilled dough makes it easier to work with.

2. Preheat the oven to 300° F. Line two baking sheets with kitchen parchment.

3. Roll out the dough on a lightly floured work surface to a thickness of about 1/2 inch. Cut out the cookies using a 2-inch round cookie cutter. Gather the scraps, re-roll and cut more cookies until the dough is gone.

4. Bake the cookies in batches until slightly puffed and firm, but not browned, 30 to 40 minutes. Cool for 10 minutes on the baking sheet, then transfer the cookies to a rack to cool completely.

Apple-Date Cake with Cajeta Crème Anglaise

SERVES 6

1	large egg
⅓	cup vegetable oil
1	teaspoon vanilla bean paste
1	teaspoon Mexican vanilla
¾	cup sugar
1	cup all-purpose flour
¼	teaspoon salt
½	teaspoon baking soda
¼	teaspoon freshly grated nutmeg
¾	teaspoon ground canela
2	peeled and diced Gala or Braeburn apples (about 1⅔ cups)
⅓	cup diced medjool dates (about 3)
⅓	cup toasted pecans, chopped

These delicious little cakes are contributed to us by our resident retailer, Susan Thomas. She loves to make them because they are so easy and delicious!

1. Preheat the oven to 350° F. Butter and flour a 2-quart rectangular baking dish.

2. Combine the egg, oil, vanilla bean paste and vanilla in a glass measuring cup. In a large bowl, whisk together the sugar, flour, salt, baking soda, nutmeg and canela. Slowly stir the liquid into the dry ingredients until everything is moistened. Add the apples, dates and pecans, and combine thoroughly with the batter. The mixture will be very thick.

3. Pour the batter into the baking dish. Bake on the center oven rack for 30 minutes. Remove from the oven and cool for 15 minutes.

4. To serve, combine 1/2 cup Cajeta with 1 cup Crème Anglaise and stir to combine. Onto each warmed dessert plate, pool 3 tablespoons of the sauce and position a piece of cake in the center.

Crème Anglaise

1   cup heavy cream
½   cup milk
1   tablespoon vanilla bean
     paste
3   large egg yolks
3   tablespoons sugar

1. Combine the cream, milk and vanilla bean paste in a medium saucepan. Bring to a simmer over low heat. Cover, remove from heat and let steep for 30 minutes.

2. Whisk the egg yolks and sugar in a small bowl. Return the milk mixture to low heat and bring to a simmer. Stirring constantly, slowly pour the egg mixture into the milk and whisk until thoroughly combined. Cook over very low heat until thick enough to coat the back of a spoon, about 8 minutes (180 to 185° on an instant-read thermometer). Strain the mixture through a fine-mesh sieve into a small bowl. Cool completely, cover with plastic wrap pressed onto the surface of the sauce and refrigerate until chilled.

Cajeta

1   quart fresh goat milk
1   cup sugar
1   stick canela
¼   teaspoon baking soda

1. Combine milk, sugar and canela in a large saucepan over medium heat. (It is important to use a large pan that will contain the mixture as it foams.) Stir regularly until the milk comes to a simmer. Remove pan from the heat and whisk in the baking soda with care, the mixture could foam and spill over the sides of the pan. When the foaming subsides, return the pan to the heat. Reduce heat and continue simmering until it reduces substantially and becomes thick and lightly golden, about 1 hour. The consistency should be that of a medium-thick caramel sauce. Stir regularly to keep the mixture from sticking.

2. Strain through a fine-mesh sieve. Keep at room temperature if using within a few hours, or refrigerate the cajeta for future use.

Phyllo Cups with Pistachios & Passion Fruit Curd

SERVES 12

PASSION FRUIT CURD

¾ **cup unsweetened passion fruit concentrate**

½ **cup plus 2 tablespoons sugar**

Pinch of salt

3 **whole eggs**

6 **egg yolks**

½ **cup (1 stick) unsalted butter, cut into tablespoon-sized pieces**

PHYLLO CUPS

Vegetable spray

6 **sheets phyllo, thawed**

4 **tablespoons melted butter**

⅓ **cup, approximately, shelled, unsalted pistachios, finely chopped**

Raw sugar

OPTIONAL GARNISHES

Mint
Toasted coconut
Fresh berries
Whipped cream

Every time these are served at parties, it never fails that at least one person requests the recipe. These are a very unusual dessert and people are always surprised at how refreshing and delicious they are. You can make everything in advance and pour the custard into the phyllo right before you serve. If you can't find the passion fruit concentrate at a local specialty store, you can use orange juice concentrate in its place.

FOR PASSION FRUIT CURD

1. Place the passion fruit concentrate, sugar, salt, whole eggs and yolks into a large bowl and whisk until the eggs have broken up and the sugar has dissolved. Make sure this bowl will fit into the top of the saucepan used in Step 2.

2. Place a large saucepan containing 2 inches of water over a high flame. Bring the water to a boil and reduce to a simmer. Add half the butter to the bowl with the first five ingredients and place the bowl in the top of the saucepan. Whisk until the butter has melted and the ingredients are warm. Whisk in the remaining butter, and continue stirring until the mixture becomes very thick. Pour the thickened mixture through a medium-mesh sieve into a nonreactive container. Press a piece of plastic wrap directly onto the surface of the curd to prevent a skin from forming and chill until ready to serve.

FOR PHYLLO CUPS

1. Preheat the oven to 375° F.

2. Lightly spray the cups of a 12-cup muffin tin with vegetable spray. Stack 6 phyllo sheets on a work surface and cut into 4-inch squares. Press one of the squares into each cup and brush each square with a little melted butter. Sprinkle with crushed pistachios and a little raw sugar. Press another square on top of the first, making sure the corners are at different angles. Brush that layer with a little butter and sprinkle with a little more raw sugar.

3. Bake until golden, about 5 to 6 minutes. Cool slightly on a wire rack and carefully remove the phyllo cups from the tins. Place the formed cups on the wire rack and continue cooling. Do not fill until ready to use.

4. When ready to serve, spoon the filling (about 2 to 3 tablespoons per cup) into the cups, garnish and serve immediately.

CREAM CHEESE PIE
WITH PINEAPPLE-COCONUT SAUCE

SERVES 12

CRUST

1¾ cups crushed shortbread cookies or vanilla wafers

4 tablespoons melted butter

2 tablespoons sugar

2 tablespoons ground canela

Pinch of salt

FILLING

12 ounces cream cheese or ricotta, at room temperature

¼ cup sugar

1 14-ounce can sweetened condensed milk

3 whole eggs

2 egg yolks

1 3-ounce can evaporated milk

1 tablespoon Mexican vanilla

4 tablespoons fresh lime juice

Pinch of salt

FOR THE CRUST

1. Preheat oven to 350° F. Position a rack in the center position.

2. Mix all crust ingredients and press evenly into a 9-inch springform pan, forming a slight (1/2 inch) lip around the edge. Bake for 6 to 8 minutes. Remove from the oven and cool.

FOR THE FILLING

1. Cut the cream cheese into 1-inch cubes and put into a blender. Add the sugar and sweetened condensed milk. Puree until smooth. Add whole eggs, yolks, evaporated milk, vanilla, lime juice and salt and blend again until smooth.

2. Pour the filling into the crust and carefully transfer to the oven. Bake for 1 hour, or until the filling is set and the surface is lightly golden and then cool. Serve each slice with a ladle of Pineapple-Coconut Sauce.

Pineapple-Coconut Sauce:

1 cup sweetened coconut
2½ cups diced fresh ripe pineapple
½ to ¾ cup sugar to taste
½ cup frozen pineapple juice concentrate, thawed
1 teaspoon ground canela
¾ cup water

1. Toast the coconut in a preheated 350° F oven until lightly browned (about 2 minutes).

2. Place all ingredients in a 2-quart saucepan. Bring to a boil, reduce heat and simmer for 15 to 20 minutes, until slightly thickened. Cool.

Farmers Market Peach & Raspberry Crisp

SERVES 8

¾ cup all-purpose flour
½ cup brown sugar
¼ teaspoon salt
½ teaspoon baking soda
1 stick or 8 tablespoons unsalted, softened butter, cut into small pieces
1 cup rolled oats
4 pounds firm, ripe peaches (8 to 10 large)
1 cup fresh raspberries

This simple dessert recipe has been a staple at the Curtis household for years, thanks to Marj Curtis, our very special mother-in-law and grandmother. It works well with many fruits such as apples and blueberries. Depending on the sweetness of the fruit, you may want to add a little sugar to the fruit.

1. Preheat the oven to 350° F. Lightly butter an 11 x 7 x 2-inch glass dish.

2. Combine the flour, sugar, salt and baking soda. Add the butter and oats to the mixture. Hand mix until well blended. Set aside.

3. If the peaches are ripe, you can peel them with a paring knife and the skins will peel off easily. If your peaches are less ripe, you may have to drop them into boiling water for about 30 seconds to make peeling easier. Slice the peeled peaches into thick wedges. Gently fold in the raspberries and pour into the prepared dish.

4. Sprinkle the topping evenly over the top of the fruit and bake for about 45 minutes to 1 hour.

Amaretto Tofu Cheesecake with Apricot Topping

SERVES 10

4	whole graham crackers
½	cup packed dried apricots, cut into quarters
2	tablespoons sliced almonds
½	teaspoon ground canela
2	cups firm silken tofu, drained
8	ounces cream cheese
¼	cup sour cream
⅔	cup sugar
2	large eggs
¼	cup amaretto

Pinch of salt

APRICOT CANELA TOPPING

1	10-ounce jar apricot preserves
⅓	cup water
2	tablespoons amaretto
1	tablespoon freshly squeezed lemon juice
½	teaspoon ground canela

OPTIONAL GARNISHES

Sliced fresh apricots
Fresh blackberries
Sliced fresh peaches
Toasted sliced almonds
Mint leaves

When Janet Mitchell brought this recipe to us for a Southwest Spa class she was developing, we cringed at the thought of a cheesecake made with tofu. However, this cheesecake is really good and was designed as a healthy alternative to a traditional cheesecake.

1. Preheat oven to 325° F. Coat an 8-inch springform pan with nonstick spray. Wrap the outside of the pan with a double thickness of aluminum foil to keep water out while the cheesecake is baking in a water bath.

2. Place graham crackers, apricots, almonds and canela in the bowl of a food processor and process until finely ground. Pour into prepared pan and press down evenly over bottom.

3. Wipe crumbs from food processor and blade, and place tofu, cream cheese, sour cream, sugar, eggs, amaretto and salt in bowl. Process until very smooth, stopping to scrape down sides of bowl as needed. Pour over crust.

4. Place cheesecake in a hollow roasting pan and pour in enough hot water to come 1 inch up the outside of the springform pan. Bake about 50 minutes, or until the edges are firm but the center still jiggles when the pan is tapped.

5. Place cheesecake on a wire rack. Run a knife around the outer edge of the cheesecake, remove foil, and let cool to room temperature before covering and refrigerating.

6. Make the topping just before serving. Combine all the topping ingredients in a small saucepan and cook, stirring, over low heat for 3 minutes, or until heated through.

7. Slice cheesecake and serve each piece with Apricot Canela Topping. Garnish with optional fruits or nuts as desired.

FIRM OR SILKEN TOFU?
Firm tofu can be thought of as your all-purpose tofu, good for grilling, frying or sautéing, but tender enough to take the place of soft tofu. If you are buying tofu but aren't actually sure what you are going to do with it, buy firm. Silken tofu is more delicate and is generally not packed in water. Silken tofu comes labeled soft, firm and extra-firm, but even the extra-firm is fairly soft. The silken tofu is ideal for pureeing and using in dishes where you plan to have it disappear. When using pureed tofu in baked goods, be sure it is completely smooth before adding it to a batter, or little bundles of tofu will appear.

Soft tofu is best for baking, or in sauces, dips, smoothies or with eggs. It has the most delicate taste and is also the most difficult to handle. Extra-firm tofu is used when you really want the tofu to hold up for something like grilling. It is coarse and lacks the delicacy of softer tofu.

POACHED PEARS WITH FRESH BERRIES

SERVES 6

SYRUP

1	bottle fruity white wine
2	cups water
½	cup sugar
Peel from 1 lemon, cut in wide strips, plus the juice	
1	stick canela
1	Mexican vanilla bean, split and scraped or 1 tablespoon vanilla paste (See page 176 to learn about vanilla)
3	to 4 pieces star anise, optional

FRUIT

3	ripe, firm Bosc, Bartlett or D'Anjou pears, stems left on, peeled, halved and cored
½	cup mixed fresh berries (strawberries, blueberries, raspberries, blackberries)
6	mint sprigs for garnish

1. For the syrup, place all the ingredients in a large saucepan and bring to a boil. Reduce the heat and simmer for 10 minutes. Add the peeled pears, bring the liquid back to a simmer and poach the pears for about 10 minutes, or until softened.

2. Remove the pears from the liquid with a slotted spoon to a plate and cool. Reduce the liquid until thick and syrupy, 10 to 15 minutes. Strain the syrup.

3. Serve the pears with a spoonful of fresh berries in the center (where the core was) and spoon the syrup over the fruit to moisten. Garnish with a sprig of mint and serve.

Star anise is the fruit of an evergreen tree native to China. It is a star-shaped, dark brown pod that contains a pea-sized seed in each of its eight segments. Although the flavor of its seeds is derived from anethol, which is the same oil that gives anise seed its pronounced flavor, they actually come from different heritage. It is slightly more bitter than regular anise seed.

Wontons de Plantano

SERVES 8 (2 PER PERSON)

WONTONS

1	cup sweetened coconut
1	banana
9	ounces chocolate chips
¼	cup milk
8	to 10 egg roll wrappers
2	cups vegetable oil

CARAMELO DE COCO Y CACHACA

¼	cup (4 tablespoons) butter
1½	cup brown sugar
½	can coconut milk
¼	cup cachaca

FOR WONTONS

1. Toast the coconut in a preheated 350° F oven until lightly browned, about 2 minutes.

2. Slice the banana into 1/2-inch slices.

2. Melt chocolate chips with milk.

3. Dip sliced bananas into chocolate, then roll in toasted coconut, place in freezer to set, about 1 hour.

4. Cut egg roll wrappers in half diagonally, place frozen banana in center of wrap, moisten edges and close.

5. Heat the oil to 375° and fry the egg roll–covered banana until golden brown. Serve with Caramelo de Coco y Cachaca.

NOTE: The wontons can be prepared ahead and frozen prior to frying.

FOR CARAMELO DE COCO Y CACHACA

1. Melt butter. Add the sugar and coconut milk and whisk.

2. Add cachaca and let sauce simmer 20 minutes.

Cachaca is a very potent Brazilian liquor made from sugarcane juice. It has recently become quite popular in the United States, but brandy can be substituted.

ROASTED TOMATILLO SALSA

NOE'S OUTRAGEOUS SOPAIPILLAS

ROASTED HABANERO PICKLED ONIONS

ORANGE-CILANTRO SALSA

GREEN CHILE PESTO

BLUE CORNMEAL BUTTERMILK BISCUITS

ODDS AND ENDS

Blue Cornmeal Buttermilk Biscuits

YIELDS 8 2-INCH
BISCUITS

1½ cups all-purpose flour

¼ cup plus 2 tablespoons blue cornmeal

2 teaspoons baking powder

¾ teaspoon baking soda

¾ teaspoon salt

1½ tablespoons sugar

6 tablespoons unsalted butter, chilled and cut into ½-inch pieces

¾ cup plus 1 tablespoon buttermilk

1. Preheat oven to 400° F.

2. Pulse flour, cornmeal, baking powder, baking soda, salt and sugar in a food processor. Add the unsalted butter and pulse until the butter pieces are the size of small peas. Pour the contents into a medium bowl and with a fork, stir in 3/4 cup buttermilk until the mixture holds together. Don't overwork the dough.

3. Line a baking sheet with parchment paper. Lightly flour a work surface and roll out the dough to a thickness of 1 inch. Using a 2-inch round cookie cutter or drinking glass, cut out 8 rounds and place on the parchment. Brush the tops of the biscuits with remaining buttermilk. Bake until golden and puffy, about 12 to 15 minutes. Serve warm with Piñon Nut Butter.

Piñon Nut Butter

½ cup (1 stick) butter, softened

1 tablespoon honey

Salt to taste

½ cup toasted piñon nuts

1. With a wooden spoon, cream butter, honey, and salt together in a small bowl.

2. Pulse piñon nuts in a food processor until fine, but not a paste.

3. Stir nuts into the butter mixture. The butter can be used immediately, or rolled into cylinders in plastic wrap and then refrigerated or frozen. Slice into rounds before serving. Piñon Nut Butter can be frozen for several weeks.

Roasted Habanero Pickled Onions

YIELDS ABOUT 4 CUPS

⅓ cup olive oil

4 medium red onions cut into thin slivers

3 bay leaves

Leaves from 6 sprigs fresh marjoram

1 teaspoon Mexican oregano

Coarsely ground black pepper to taste

Freshly ground allspice to taste

½ cup balsamic or red wine vinegar

6 fresh habanero chiles, roasted and chopped

Salt to taste

These onions are a great condiment to keep in your refrigerator. We serve these with our fajitas, but they would also be tasty on sandwiches or melted cheese hors d'oeuvres. It is really best to let these marinate for 6 to 8 hours; we just don't have the time in our 3-hour classes to marinate that long. They will keep for up to a month in the refrigerator.

1. Heat the oil in a large skillet over high heat. Lightly sauté the onions and the bay leaves for 4 to 5 minutes, or until lightly golden on the edges. Remove from heat and stir in the marjoram, oregano, pepper and allspice, and combine thoroughly.

2. Stir in the vinegar and habaneros and season with salt to taste. Set aside for at least 30 minutes or longer. Serve at room temperature or chilled.

Orange-Cilantro Salsa

SERVES 6

3 large oranges, peeled and sectioned

2 large ruby grapefruits, peeled and sectioned

1 large bunch cilantro, roughly chopped

1 or 2 serrano chiles, minced

1 red onion, trimmed and cut into slivers

Extra virgin olive oil to taste

Balsamic or red wine vinegar to taste

Salt to taste

Combine the ingredients and mix well. Set aside for 20 minutes. Taste and adjust seasonings.

Spicy Roasted Onions

SERVES 6 OR MORE

2 pounds red or yellow onions

¼ cup olive oil

10 fresh sage leaves or 1 teaspoon dried

6 thyme branches or ½ teaspoon dried

1 teaspoon freshly ground black pepper

½ cup balsamic vinegar

2 tablespoons chopped parsley

These roasted onions work well as a side dish for many different menus. They are good served hot, cold or at room temperature.

1. Preheat oven to 375° F. Lightly butter or oil a large baking pan.

2. Peel onions and slice into 1/2-inch rounds, separate rings, and toss with remaining ingredients except parsley.

3. Spread seasoned onions in prepared pan, cover with foil, and bake for 30 minutes.

4. Remove foil, stir onions, cover, and bake for an additional 15 minutes more. Uncover, stir again, and return to oven for another 15 minutes, or until juices are syrupy. Top with parsley just before serving.

Roasted Poblano Sauce

YIELDS 1½ TO 2 CUPS

4 poblano chiles, roasted, peeled and seeded

½ bunch cilantro

4 cloves garlic, roasted and peeled

¼ cup yellow onion, sautéed

2 to 3 tablespoons honey

¼ cup olive oil

1 tablespoon fresh lime juice (optional)

Salt and pepper to taste

This green chile sauce variation was originally served with our tamale bonus class. All of our chefs had a slightly different take on the recipe, but this is the one we liked the best.

1. Place chiles, cilantro, garlic, onion and honey in blender. With motor running, slowly drizzle in olive oil.

2. Adjust seasonings with lime juice, salt and pepper.

ΠOE'S OUTRAGEOUS SOPAIPILLAS

**YIELDS ABOUT 10 TO 12
SOPAIPILLAS**

1   cup all-purpose flour
½   teaspoon salt
¾   teaspoon baking powder
1   tablespoon sugar
2   teaspoons vegetable
    shortening
½   cup buttermilk
1   teaspoon vanilla paste
Canola oil for frying

Noe Cano, long-time kitchen manager and sous chef at the school, developed this version of sopaipillas, which are standard fare in most traditional New Mexico restaurants. These are so light and fluffy they just melt in your mouth. The buttermilk causes the sopaipillas to puff up, but the vanilla paste adds a wonderful flavor. You really don't need the honey and butter that are typically served with sopaipillas.

1. Combine the flour, salt, baking powder and sugar in a bowl. Cut in the shortening until a coarse meal is formed. Stir in the buttermilk and vanilla paste with a fork until the mixture comes together into a moist dough. Form into a ball, knead several times, and cover; let the dough rest for 30 minutes.

2. Heat the oil in a deep pot to 375° F. Roll out half the dough to 1/8 inch thickness and cut into squares or triangles. Drop the pieces of dough, one by one, into the hot oil and fry until golden, about 30 to 40 seconds, rolling them over to brown on both sides. Roll and cut remaining dough and fry. Drain on paper towels and serve warm with honey or honey butter, if desired. See Technique of Making Sopaipillas on page 202.

For a richer flavor and more interesting texture, you can substitute 1/4 cup panocha flour for the white flour (panocha is a coarsely ground whole wheat flour).

TECHNIQUE OF MAKING SOPAIPILLAS

1. Roll the sopaipilla dough into a large rectangle about 1/8 inch thick.

2. Cut the rolled dough into large squares.

3. Add a few of the dough squares to the heated oil and spoon the hot oil over the dough to help it puff.

4. Fry the squares until puffed and golden on both sides and repeat with any remaining squares.

Green Chile Pesto

YIELDS 2 TO 2½ CUPS

1½ cups roasted green chile, peeled and seeded

½ cup toasted piñon nuts

6 cloves roasted garlic

¼ cup grated parmesan cheese

¼ cup olive oil

Salt and pepper to taste

Combine chile, piñon nuts, garlic and cheese in the work bowl of a food processor and pulse to combine. With motor running, drizzle in oil. Adjust seasoning with salt and pepper.

Roasted Tomatillo Salsa

YIELDS 2 CUPS

1 pound tomatillos (7 or 8 medium), soaked, husked and dried

2 or 3 fresh serrano chiles, stemmed

1 small white onion, peeled and sliced ½ inch thick

2 or 3 garlic cloves, peeled

½ cup water (or as needed)

⅓ cup chopped fresh cilantro

1 teaspoon kosher salt or to taste

1 teaspoon sugar (optional)

1. Heat the broiler. Lay the tomatillos and serranos on a baking sheet. Set the sheetpan 4 inches below the broiler and roast the tomatillos until softened and splotchy black in places, about 5 minutes. Turn the tomatillos and chiles and roast the other side for another 4 to 5 minutes. Set aside to cool.

2. Reduce heat to 400° F. Separate the onion into rings. On a baking sheet, combine the onion and garlic. Roast the onion mixture, stirring carefully every couple of minutes, until the onions are browned. The garlic should feel soft and be browned in spots. Total roasting time will be about 15 minutes. Cool to room temperature.

3. By hand, coarsely chop the onion-garlic mixture and the roasted serrano chiles and place in a medium bowl.

4. Coarsely puree the tomatillos with their juice in the food processor and add the puree to the onion-garlic-chile mixture. Stir in enough water to give the salsa a slightly thick, but spoonable, consistency. Stir in the cilantro. Taste and season with salt and sugar.

TECHNIQUE OF MAKING CORN TORTILLAS

1. Cut two rounds of plastic from a plastic baggie to line the inside of the tortilla press and place one of the rounds on the bottom surface of the press. Place a ball of the tortilla masa onto the plastic in the center of the press.

2. Place the second round of plastic over the ball, flattening it slightly.

3. Fold the top of the press over and flatten the masa into a thin round.

4. Remove the tortilla from the press and carefully peel one side of the plastic from the masa. Flip the tortilla over and carefully remove the plastic from the other side.

5. Place the tortillas on a preheated griddle with no oil and cook on one side until lightly browned in spots. Turn the tortillas and continue to brown on the other side. Remove the toasted tortillas to a warming basket.

YIELD: 16 4-INCH TORTILLAS

2   cups masa harina
½   teaspoon salt
1⅓ cups (approximately) warm
     water

Place the dry ingredients in a
medium bowl and slowly add the
water, stirring with a fork until
the dough comes together into a
ball. Knead the dough several
times and roll into a log shape
about 2 inches in diameter and
8 inches long. Wrap the log in
plastic wrap and let it stand for
about 30 minutes.

Preheat a cast iron comal, skillet
or griddle over medium-high heat.
Cut the log into 1/2-inch rounds,
keeping them covered so the dough
doesn't dry out. Follow the step by
step technique of making tortillas.

Caipirinha Punch

SERVES 8 TO 10

4   lemons
4   limes
1   cup dry white wine
1   cup agave wine
1   cup sugar
1   liter lemon/lime soda
Ice (as needed)

Known as Brazil's national drink, this version was created by Carmen Rodriguez for our Carnaval class. In Brazil, it is typically made with cachaca, a potent brandy made from sugarcane. We have substituted agave wine and have had rave reviews.

1. Cut lemons and limes into eighths and place in a large pitcher.
2. Crush citrus with a wooden pestle or the back of a wooden spoon. Add both wines and sugar and stir until sugar dissolves.
3. Add lemon/lime soda.
4. Pour over ice and garnish with sliced limes or lemons.

Gringo Mole

YIELDS 2 TO 2½ CUPS

3   yellow bell peppers, roasted and seeded
2   jalapeños, roasted, peeled and seeded
3   tablespoons sesame seeds, toasted
1   tablespoon honey
¼   cup peanut oil
Salt and pepper to taste

Combine peppers, jalapeños, sesame seeds and honey in a blender and puree until smooth. With motor running, drizzle in oil. Season with salt and pepper.

Bayless, Rick. *Mexico One Plate At A Time.* New York: Charles Scribner, 2000.

Bayless, Rick. *Rick Bayless's Mexican Kitchen.* New York: Charles Scribner, 1996.

Brenner, Leslie and Lettie Teague. *Fear of Wine: An Introductory Guide To the Grape.* New York: Bantam Books, 1995.

Brown-Martinez, Nancy. *Origins of Wine & Beer in New Mexico: A Brief History.* Belen, New Mexico: Spanish History Publications, 2003.

Caruso, James Campbell. *El Farol: Tapas and Spanish Cuisine.* Salt Lake City, Utah: Gibbs Smith, Publisher, 2004.

Casas, Penelope. *Tapas: The Little Dishes of Spain.* New York: Alfred A. Knopf, 2003.

Curtis, Susan. *The Santa Fe School of Cooking Cookbook.* Salt Lake City, Utah: Gibbs Smith, Publisher, 1995.

Dent, Huntley. *The Feast of Santa Fe.* New York: Simon & Schuster, Inc.,1985.

Dewitt, Dave and Nancy Gerlach. *Just North of the Border.* Albuquerque, New Mexico: Out West Publishing, 1989.

DeWitt, Dave and Nancy Gerlach. *The Whole Chile Pepper Book.* New York: Little, Brown and Company, 1990.

Gilbert, Fabiola C. *Historic Cookery.* Las Vegas, New Mexico: La Galeria de los Artesanos, 1970.

Harrison, Babs Suzanne and Staefan Edvard Rada. *Exploring New Mexico Wine Country.* Los Cerrillos, New Mexico: Coyote Press, 1994.

Herbst, Sharon Tyler. *Food Lover's Companion.* New York: Barron's Educational Series Inc., 2001.

Jamison, Cheryl Alters and Bill Jamison. *American Home Cooking.* New York: Broadway Books, 1999.

Jamison, Cheryl Alters and Bill Jamison. *The Border Cookbook.* Boston: Harvard Common Press, 1995.

Kennedy, Diana. *From My Mexican Kitchen.* New York: Random House, 2003.

Madison, Deborah. *Local Flavors.* New York: Broadway Books, 2002.

Madison, Deborah. *This Can't Be Tofu.* New York: Broadway Books, 2000.

Madison, Deborah. *Vegetarian Cooking for Everyone.* New York: Broadway Books, 1997.

Miller, Mark. *Coyote Café.* Berkeley, California: Ten Speed Press, 1989.

Miller, Mark. *The Great Chile Book.* Berkeley: Ten Speed Press, 1991.

Miller, Mark, Stephan Pyles and John Sedlar. *Tamales.* New York: MacMillan, 1997.

Quintana, Patricia. *Mexico's Feasts of Life.* Tulsa, Oklahoma: Council Oak Books, 1989.

Werle, Loukie and Jill Cox. *Ingredients.* Australia: JB Fairfax Press, 2000.

Typical Classes at the Cooking School

"I use my oven for storage," says one student, a woman from Chicago, at the beginning of a Contemporary Southwest I class, and her friends, sitting around her, chuckle knowingly. All classes at The Santa Fe School of Cooking, whether it's Southwestern Barbecue class for twenty-five or a salsa-making contest for a private group, begin with casual introductions: first the instructor and staff, then the students. "No worries," says Rocky Durham, an internationally acclaimed chef who has taught at the school for more than a decade, "You've come to the right place."

Indeed, over the course of about two hours, as Rocky demonstrates how to make a three-course meal that includes lime-marinated salmon with ginger lime butter and salsa with roasted corn, tomato and black beans, he infuses confidence into the students, whether they're novices or professionals.

While showing the class how to roast a green chile (char the skin as quickly as possible over a gas stove) and create the delicious marinade (throw jalapeños, limes and cilantro, skin, stems and all, and a dash of oil into a Cuisinart), Rocky hits on various aspects of the culinary world, both practical and philosophical.

He illustrates how to efficiently slice an onion and chop cilantro; he explains how to justify mistakes ("If something doesn't come out how you expected, call it something else"); he expounds on the intricacies of the state's most misunderstood fruit, the chile. "Only talking about the heat of a chile is like only referring to the alcohol content of a wine grape," he says, passionately, "There's so much more flavor to consider." Once the appetizing meal, accompanied by locally produced beer, wine and soda, is served, Rocky, a native of Santa Fe, gives recommendations of the best restaurants, along with some childhood autobiographical details. "Every dish my mother made included cheese, bread crumbs and potato chips in a Pyrex dish," he says with a laugh. Fortunately, his palate has since matured considerably.

While all of the school's nine chefs lend their own flavor to their classes—Rocky's wit is matched by Kathi's attention to detail and Daniel's informative stories— what is consistent among the instruction is the dedication to passing on the local culinary traditions in an authentic, accessible manner. Just as importantly, the chefs inspire students to return home and create their own blue corn muffins or anise poundcakes. Our proof? The hundreds of graduation diplomas we've sent out over the years; you officially graduate from the school once you make a southwestern dish at home and then send a picture of it to us. We loved the enthusiasm from one of our graduates as she mailed back the entire dinner she prepared; however, it is really only necessary (and encouraged) to send a photo! While we haven't yet received a picture from the student whose oven was a storage facility, if history is any indication, it will soon be on its way.

Sources for Southwestern Ingredients

Santa Fe School of Cooking and Market
116 West San Francisco Street
Santa Fe, NM 87501
(800) 982-4688
www.santafeschoolofcooking.com

Large variety of dried chiles, chile seeds, full range of New Mexican and Southwestern ingredients and seasonings, Southwestern cooking equipment. Catalog available.

Leona's De Chimayo
PO Box 579
Chimayo, NM 87522
(888) 561-5569
www.leonasrestaurante.com

Tortillas. Traditional flour, whole wheat and flavored. Tamales.

Sweetwoods Dairy
PO Box 1238
Pena Blanca, NM 87041
(505) 465-2608

Goat cheese made fresh daily. Plain and herb-flavored.

Native Seeds/SEARCH
526 North 4th Avenue
Tucson, AZ 85705
(866) 622-5561
www.nativeseeds.org

Variety of seeds of the Southwestern Native American Crops.

Maple Leaf Farms
www.mapleleaffarms.com

Provides high quality duck products.

The Santa Fe School of Cooking has an adjoining market where we sell over 600 products, most of which are made in New Mexico. We sell everything from chile powder, posole and blue corn meal to salsa, ceramics, cookbooks and aprons. Many people use it as their resource for hard-to-find southwestern ingredients. Products can be ordered over the phone, via the mail or the Internet.

1-800-982-4688
www.santafeschooolofcooking.com